MASTER
NEGATIVE
NO. 91-80174-2

COLUMBIA UNIVERSITY LIBRARIES
PRESERVATION DEPARTMENT

BIBLIOGRAPHIC MICROFORM TARGET

Original Material as Filmed - Existing Bibliographic Record

113
R191

Rawson, Frederick Lawrence, 1859-)°°°.

Life understood from a scientific and religious point of
view, and the practical method of destroying sin, disease, and
death. By F. L. Rawson ... 2d ed. London, The Crystal
press, ltd., 1914.

xvi, 4, 4a-4e, (1, 4e-4e, (5,-740 p. 1 l. front. (port.) 22ᶜᵐ.

1. Cosmology—Curiosa and miscellany. 2. New thought. I. Title.

35-15982

Library of Congress   BD701.R3 1914

Restrictions on Use:

TECHNICAL MICROFORM DATA

FILM SIZE: 35 ____   REDUCTION RATIO: 11✗
IMAGE PLACEMENT: IA IIA IB IIB
DATE FILMED: 8/7/91   INITIALS RK
FILMED BY: RESEARCH PUBLICATIONS, INC WOODBRIDGE, CT

AIIM

Association for Information and Image Management

1100 Wayne Avenue, Suite 1100
Silver Spring, Maryland 20910

301/587-8202

Centimeter

1 2 3 4 5 6 7 8 9 10 11 12 13 14 15 mm

Inches

1.0	2.8	2.5
1.1	3.2	2.2
	3.6	2.0
		1.8
1.25	1.4	1.6

MANUFACTURED TO AIIM STANDARDS

BY APPLIED IMAGE, INC.

Presented to
Mehitabel Crawford
by her good
friend
Mrs Boynton
N. Y.
Xmas. 1917.

LIFE UNDERSTOOD

Yours sincerely
F. L. Rawson

LIFE UNDERSTOOD

FROM A SCIENTIFIC AND RELIGIOUS POINT OF VIEW,

AND

THE PRACTICAL METHOD OF DESTROYING

SIN, DISEASE, AND DEATH

By F. L. RAWSON,

*Member of the Institution of Electrical Engineers and London
Member of the Institution of Civil Engineers; Consulting Engineer
to the Government of Ireland; Past Member of Council and some-
time President of the London Association; and past Vice-
President of the Astronomical Institute; Author of
"Experience in Prayer," and "Power," and the
"Reasonury Dictionary," for the Hymn-
book, "Material and if Any
Means; What It Is," &c.
St. Alongius Agnen
etc. etc. etc.*

SECOND EDITION

LONDON

THE CRYSTAL PRESS, LIMITED,

8, REGENT STREET, W.

1914

Yours sincerely,
F. L. Rawson

LIFE UNDERSTOOD

FROM A SCIENTIFIC AND RELIGIOUS POINT OF VIEW,

AND

THE PRACTICAL METHOD OF DESTROYING

SIN, DISEASE, AND DEATH.

By F. L. RAWSON,

Member of the Institution of Electrical Engineers and Associate Member of the Institution of Civil Engineers; Consulting Engineer to the Government of Ireland; Hon. Member of Council and past Vice-President of the Aëroplane Association; and past Vice-President of the Aëronautical Institute. Author of Articles on "Present" and "Future," and the "Engineers' Dictionary," for the Harmsworth "Education"; and of "Aëroplanes: What It Is," for the Aëroplane Association; and other works.

SECOND EDITION.

LONDON:
THE CRYSTAL PRESS, LIMITED,
90, REGENT STREET, W.
1914.

Dedicated to

MY BROTHERS AND SISTERS, THE MASS OF MANKIND,
WRITHING UNDER THE LASH OF FALSE LAWS,
THROUGH IGNORANCE OF TRUTH.

INDEX OF CONTENTS.

PREFACE TO THE SECOND EDITION.

I HAVE to thank many readers of the first edition who have written to me, giving me details of how, by putting into practice the truths stated, they have, to their great joy, been able to help, not only themselves, but their fellow-beings, in a number of instances and in a great variety of ways. This is the natural outcome of true religion, when wedded to true science, and should be our sole aim in this world of agonising suffering. There is no proof of any theory but results. God is the great I am, Life, Truth, Love, Mind, Soul, Spirit, cause, all substance, and intelligence, and therefore the Principle of good. This divine Principle, omnipotent and universal, inevitably and instantly works, destroying evil, if a man, even for a moment, stops thinking wrongly and thinks rightly. God being no respecter of persons, hears the prayers of a sinner just as much as those of a saint, if only the sinner prays rightly, that is, in accordance with divine rule or Principle.

Our great need is to know what constitutes true prayer. For countless centuries man has endeavoured to solve the mystery of life, and for nearly 2,000 years he has struggled to know the truth, the truth that Jesus declared would set man free. This knowledge of the truth is knowledge of God and leads to true prayer, conscious communion with God.

The Right and Wrong Methods of Prayer.—

The value of "Life Understood" is not to prove that all disease is mental, as medical men are rapidly coming to this conclusion; nor is it to prove that matter is mental phenomena, and can be caused to appear and disappear by thought, although the scientific difference between the two methods in which this can be done is given. One is the fatal and exhausting way in which the witches and sorcerers of olden times, and black magic workers and hypnotists of the present day work, namely, with the human mind, which inevitably leads to sin, disease, and death; the other is the marvellous and inspiring way in which Jesus the Christ worked, namely, by turning in thought to God, thus steadily revealing infinite health, holiness, and happiness.

The value of this book is to enable the reader to demonstrate daily what true prayer is. It shows demonstrably what God is. It lays bare and scatters to the winds the mistaken theories of natural science. It sets out exactly the difference between the right and wrong method of mentally working, as now proved by thousands of workers. It gives the scientific proofs of this difference, and shows clearly how every one can work in the right way. This is of vital importance, as in two to three years' time every intelligent person will be a mental worker. Advanced thinkers of all classes are now investigating the effect of thought and getting wonderful results, and in a year or two, at latest, the reports of their investigations will be made public, confirming beyond a shadow of doubt the most important of the statements put forward herein.

There is a hard and fast line drawn between the two methods of mentally working, and Jesus pointed out the difference more than once. If, when you are praying you are thinking of reality, that is of God or heaven, of the Christ or the spiritual man, you are helping your patient, yourself, and the world. If, on the contrary, you are thinking of the material man or the material world—whatever you may be thinking about them—you are harming your patient, harming yourself, and doing no good to the world. Even by strong determined thinking or will power you can neither destroy the evil thoughts that attack you or others nor purify the so-called human mind; you merely alter the electrical tension of what is scientifically spoken of as the lines of force of which the other is composed. Troubles invariably follow. God, namely, Truth and Love, the Principle of all good, alone heals, and this by destroying the so-called cause of the evil, under its name of the devil in theology; the other in the scientific world, and mortal mind amongst the metaphysical sects. Although few recognise it, these are the same as the unconscious or subconscious mind, subliminal self, etc., of the modern psychologist.

The Great Change in the Mental Outlook.—

When the first edition of "Life Understood" was issued, I knew that the loosing of the devil—spoken of in Revelation, and referred to in Esdras as the death of "my Son Christ"—took place in 1910, and that the terrible troubles foretold in the Bible and elsewhere would start three and a-half years later, namely, in 1914. Although I drew

attention, in Appendix XII., to the final seven years of evil, and in Appendix VIII. showed that there was war with Germany in the immediate future, to have openly stated at that time all that the Bible showed, or even what I now say, would have done more harm than good, as, with most people, it would have detracted from the value of the other facts put forward. The world was not ready. It was still on a material basis, and it was too much trouble to look into the statements made and to test whether they were true or not. Most people were too busily engaged in trying to make both ends meet. Nevertheless, in many of my lectures many details of forthcoming events were publicly given, for instance, that the serious troubles were going to start in July, 1914. I even sometimes said that the end of the world, that is the end of all sin, disease, troubles, limitations, and death itself, would take place in 1917, when all mankind would wake up to find themselves perfect beings in a perfect world, governed by a perfect God.

Since the first edition was issued, many of the new views therein presented have been confirmed. The final war has also started, and is widely recognised as one view of the battle of Armageddon, namely, its material presentation, full details of which are prophesied in the Bible. Many of these I have recently given in "How the War Will End," which also gives most of the known accurate secular prophecies. Fear of impending evil is also turning men to God. A large number of those who heard me, together with many advanced thinkers, are therefore now prepared to accept as correct what the Bible prophecies tell us with regard to the end of the world, and it is possible to be more open, especially to those, such as my readers, whose study has led them to investigate along the advanced lines of thought herein dealt with.

A great change has taken place since the first edition of "Life Understood" was published. The recognition of pseudo-mental power of mortal mind and of the Truth that sets man free has been increasing with great rapidity.

The change that has taken place during the last four years has been greater than the previous eight; that during the last two years greater than that during the previous four; in the course of the last year important changes have taken place more than all those in the previous two years. In the last six months there have been great alterations in the views of the advanced general public, and the last three months have seen even greater changes than

have taken place in the last six months. These changes will
continue with increasing rapidity, until in the last few hours of this
material sense of existence the transformation will be unparalleled
and spontaneous. These changes have taken place in England, and
also to a lesser extent in other countries, and will gradually spread
out from England and America into all civilised countries.

The So-called End of the World.—

When I prepared the second edition of "Life Understood," I
thought it better not to state definitely the details of what was
foretold with regard to the end of the world. Even when it was
finished and in the printer's hands, I thought that it was wiser to
give no details in this Preface. The tremendous change which
has taken place during the last three months, however, has shown
that the world is now ready not only to receive the information,
but, irrespective of beliefs in any particular form of religion and in
its creeds and dogmas, to pray persistently in the scientific manner
taught and demonstrated by Jesus the Christ, with a view of
relieving the suffering that now exists and the suffering that
admittedly in any case must continue to make this earth a hell to
so many for some little time to come.

The end of the material world, that is, the end of all
matter, and its consequent sin, disease, troubles, worries,
and limitations, is, fortunately, close at hand, and the
scientific reasons are easy to understand. The action of God starts
the movement, and then all matter short-circuits itself. The
approximate year I first calculated out over twelve years ago,
taking as my basis the yearly increasing number of those that
knew that matter was not a reality, the only reality being God
and His manifestation. Six or seven years later, when I learnt
what I knew of the science of numbers, I was able to so
work out mathematically the exact year and month, which later
I found were shown in the Bible. Jesus only told us that we
should not know the day or the hour, and of these only an
approximate estimate can be made, as it depends upon how people
do their work at the end.

The one objection that has been put forward to this speedy
termination of all matter, and, therefore, of all evil, is that
everyone would have to be almost perfect before the end could
come. This is true, but with the large majority the vision of
perfection which brings this about comes only in the last few

minutes. The action of God, taking place through the minority,
leavens "the whole lump." The weight of thought of many millions
of the majority amounts to little, as they can hardly even be called
thinkers; whereas the power of Truth through the thought of the
trained mental worker is incalculable, because it is the power of
God, infinite good, working through the human being as through a
channel, annihilating the sense of evil.

The Bible shows that this glorious revolution, this universal
deliverance from a bondage almost unbearable to many, comes from
the united joyous effort, on a fixed and definite day, of all the
mental workers who work in the right way, namely, in the scientific
method taught and demonstrated by Jesus the Christ. This, as
shown in Daniel, results in the widespread use of "the denial"—
the great Prince Michael—by all intelligent people throughout the
world at a pre-determined date, namely, shortly after this final
war, the material battle of Armageddon, is ended. The Book of
Revelation gives many of the details, more than any other book.
II. Esdras gives many minute details, and shows definitely the
year and the month. It also gives December 3rd, 1917, as the
day on which takes place what is described by John as, "I saw
another angel flying in the midst of heaven, having the everlasting
gospel to preach unto them that dwell on the earth, and to every
nation, and kindred, and tongue, and people." The statement in
Esdras, showing exactly the time, came to me at another confirmation of what I already knew well. Note AA, on page 682, shows
how I gradually learnt the facts in connection with the end, and
page 672 gives the confirmatory statement in II. Esdras.

The Date of the End of all Matter and Evil.—

On December 3rd, 1917, as a result of the united action of the
advanced mental workers throughout the world, a circular, carefully
prepared by the leaders, is delivered, as the Apocalypse shows, in
every inhabited house, in every civilised country. It also appears
in every newspaper on that day. This is the news referred to by
Jesus as follows: "This gospel of the kingdom shall be preached
in all the world for a witness unto all nations; and then shall the
end come."

This circular, in a simple and concise way, sets out the facts of
being, and gives the verified proofs thereof. It shows the glorious
time that is at hand, and ends by calling upon everyone to unite in
turning in thought to God, and realising as clearly as possible that

there is nothing his God; in other words, that there is no reality in matter, "All is Infinite Mind and its infinite manifestation."

The denial of the reality of matter, and therefore of all evil, results in such a mental revolution that all true mental workers will that day heal practically everything instantaneously. They can even what is called "raise from the dead," and in the afternoon and evening, as shown in several of the prophetical books, the coming to life of those who are ready for burial will be quite common. Post-mortem decomposition shows whether the human mind has passed into another state of consciousness, and until then the so-called dead can be awakened up from what is only, as Jesus pointed out, a deep sleep or state of coma (see "Raising from the Dead," page 178).

On Tuesday morning there will be hardly anything else in the papers but the details of the so-called miracles that have taken place on the Monday, particulars of which their staffs have collected. The Book of Revelation shows that they will say that what is stated in the circular is true, that the realm of matter "is fallen, is fallen" and that a glorious world, "a new heaven and a new earth," is rapidly opening to our view through the destruction "for ever and ever" of the material sense that hides it from us.

On Tuesday, such is the effect produced, that the raising of "the dead (so-called), small and great," becomes universal. This sets the final seal on our false beliefs, and even the selfish materialist, who has previously scoffed at any idea of an existing spiritual world around us, hidden by the senses, will mentally work his hardest in the hope that the good news may be true, and that he will shortly be ushered from the living hell in which he has been existing during the previous six months, and may wake up to find himself in a perfect state of existence.

Then the end comes, and, as John puts it, "death and hell were cast into the lake of fire"—purified out of existence—with whatsoever "was not found written in the book of life"—existing in the world of reality.

The Forthcoming Troubles.—

All the prophets and all modern leaders of thought have foretold the troubles, in fact, the horrors, that are coming as a prelude to the end of the belief in matter. The signs of some are so evident that they are now being foreseen by scientific men and experts. They will punish us because, instead of obeying the covenant set

out by Moses, and having only one God, absolute good, and being constantly in conscious communion with God—thinking of good—we are constantly thinking wrongly, being attacked by devilish thoughts, which in the past we have intensified instead of destroyed.

Hitherto, fortunately, the thoughts have not been strong enough for the results immediately to follow. When everyone recognises the effect of so-called thought, conditions entirely change, and a thought of evil instantly brings dire punishment.

It does not do to dwell upon the troubles that are coming, because by so doing they are made worse, but details of a few are given herein. When the thought of these evils or of the suffering of the victims of the terrible war now devastating Europe comes to me, a burst of joyous feeling at once takes its place, as, with overflowing gratitude to God, I recognise that all sorrows are shortly finished for ever.

Our Work in the Meantime.—

We cannot hasten or delay the final end of all evil by even a day, but what we can do is to reduce the amount of suffering between now and that date. "The night cometh when no man can work," which means that if a man allows too much time to pass before he learns how to think rightly, the golden opportunity has been lost; and, when he wants to learn, the evil is too intense. He then has to suffer unless someone more fortunate comes to his aid. Even now, a mental worker, when the evil is too great, cannot properly protect himself, and has to seek help. At the end, so busy will all true workers be in relieving the suffering around them, that the sluggard may have to solve the problem himself, suffering the tortures of the damned, until he reaches the true idea of the Principle at work.

What each of us has to do is to learn how to think rightly, systematically, that is to say, how to pray in a scientific manner, in the way that Jesus the Master taught and demonstrated, which way is clearly set out herein. In this way, not only can we protect ourselves, and those who are near and dear to us, when the evil time comes, but as wide a circle of others as possible. Love it is that enables us, in fact, causes us to do this. Love is, and always has been, the only power. This recognised and demonstrated, is the solution of life.

The Bible refers, under different names, to the two-edged sword of truth, by which we can protect ourselves against these fiendish thoughts. One edge is what is called "the denial"—the denial of the existence of the evil in heaven—whereby the wrong thoughts, causing the trouble are destroyed. The second is the affirmation—the realisation, or dwelling in thought, on the opposite good in heaven—whereby the so-called human mind is purified by the action of God, so each time making it less susceptible thereafter to the action of the wrong thoughts, until, ultimately, they have no effect whatever.

I have been interested to see that those most ready to adopt the view that I have taken have been advanced mental workers who, by their results prove their understanding of the effect of thought, and good business men, who are, as a rule, logical thinkers, although until recently it has been difficult to get them to give the necessary time to prove the facts for themselves, and come into the firing line. Some of these have, of their own accord, seen the logical conclusion, and said to me that, if what was stated were true, the end of matter must come in a very short time, and that meant the end of all evil. Both classes have offered their fullest assistance. Naturally, such a result is only obtained by united, concerted action, as set out on pages 100 and 301 herein, and I shall be glad to hear from those who are prepared to take part in the final work that will be necessary throughout the civilised countries of the world.

After a laborious day in her hospital, the rest of Sister Dora was constantly broken by the sound of a bell which rang at the head of her bed when any sufferer required her. On that bell was engraved: "The Master is come and calleth for thee."

Our Master is calling now. "The Father seeketh such to worship him . . . in spirit and in truth."

November 21st, 1914.

"Life Understood" was published in 1912, but the original preface was dated December, 1913, which date was not afterwards altered as it marked the year from which certain statements in the body of the work must be reckoned.

In order to bring the work up to date I have had in many places to add further matter as well as footnotes. This has caused the pages to vary in length and has necessitated the addition of extra pages distinguished only by letters of the alphabet. Otherwise it would have been necessary to alter the whole of the cross references. Even as it is it has been impossible to give the time to these cross references that they deserve.

In the second edition hundreds of alterations and additions have been made, and over 70 fresh pages added, whilst Mrs. Bill's notes on Christ and Christmas have been printed at her request. She has also asked me to state that she has which no part in the preparation of the second edition. In order that practitioners and students, having different editions, can refer to necessary previous without trouble, the numbering of the pages end of the lines has been kept as in the first edition. In many places for this reason the lines have had to be crowded together.

NOTES TO READERS.

This presentation of facts does not pretend to be a collection of original discoveries, nor is it a polished literary work. It is a gathering together of the latest scientific, religious, and philosophical discoveries, a technical statement of facts reviewed in the light of the great truth that is now breaking in upon a waiting and wondering world, weary of useless theories and sick of speculative hypotheses.

The main points dealt with were touched upon, more or less fully, in a lecture delivered on August 18th, 1909. Having been asked to revise this for publication, I commenced to amplify it. As the work progressed, it was found necessary to give facts and to further elaborate and treat in detail the logical sequence of thought in order to show the accuracy of the statements made. The fact that the work has had to be done when already the whole of the day was taken up with important professional duties, has rendered it impossible to do more than present a mere succession of statements, which make no claim to literary merit. "Variety of language or beauty of diction must give place to close analysis and unembellished thought" under such circumstances.

In dealing with such infinite and vital subjects as God and man and the universe, it is essential to preserve a sense of order, and state apparent difficulties, before presenting their remedy. For this reason I would ask the reader to spend no time upon such points in the first section as are already known to him. On a second reading more attention may be given to this portion, the value of which will then be better recognised.

Some may complain of the positiveness with which most of the statements of fact are made. Time alone will prove to most people whether they are correct or not.

Any hesitation in accepting the facts herein set forth will be found to give way when these are submitted to the test of the action of the unalterable laws upon which they are based. It is within the power of each reader to demonstrate for himself the truth of such facts by application of the rules as stated.

I can promise that no regrets will follow any time spent in study of the laws referred to, when followed by practice of the habits of thought to which attention is directed.

I feel sure that the Principle which has been followed throughout, will be sufficient to provide a logical solution of any difficulty, raised by the simplest or deepest thinkers, in either the scientific or religious worlds, in connection with the vast subjects dealt with.

The reason for giving many of the quotations throughout this work is not for the purpose of proof, but to show how earnestly great thinkers, of past and present times, have been and are now reaching out in search of a scientific basis of knowledge, an unalterable Principle upon which they could absolutely rely. I will be grateful for any better quotations forthcoming as a result of this publication of facts.

Unfortunately, in a few cases references cannot be given to the writers, as the quotations are taken from miscellaneous notes made in the past. In a few instances also I cannot even be quite sure whether the words are my own notes or extracts from books read. I have also failed in many cases to give the writers' qualifications, and shall be grateful for any particulars which will enable me in a future edition to give credit where credit is due, or will allow readers to verify such quotations for themselves. In places, phrases are shown as quotations without a reference to the known author, and so this for reasons that will be appreciated as the book is read and its motives discerned.

Numerous quotations from the Bible are also given, as many of the most earnest thinkers naturally value confirmation of every truth from this source. Those who have had Christianity so put before them that their logical minds will not allow them to adopt mis-stated truths, may think that such references are too frequent. I hope that a large and important body of thinkers will bear with this owing to the fact that there are so many who are helped by such confirmatory quotations. Each can, if he prefers, pass them over, and apply his whole attention to discover the truth as otherwise expressed. On

reading through a second time, however, such readers will find in these Bible quotations an unexpected witness to every statement of truth that has been put forward. It should be clearly understood, however, that the scientific facts set forth, in no way depend upon even this most valuable testimony, as they are facts which are based upon no written statement, but rest upon an unalterable Principle. They are demonstrable living truths, which will lift the reader away from the mere field of material battle, where evil is unmasked only to be destroyed, into the spiritual realm of harmonious reality. This kingdom, for which we are all looking, is the new heaven and the new earth, the world of reality, which is merely waiting man's recognition and acceptance.

LIFE UNDERSTOOD

From a Scientific and Religious Point of View,
and the
Practical Method of Destroying Sin, Disease, and Death.

By F. L. RAWSON, M.I.E.E., A.M.I.C.E.

AMPLIFICATION OF A LECTURE DELIVERED AT LETCHWORTH,
ON AUGUST 16TH, 1909.

"Science is bound by the everlasting law of honour to face fearlessly every problem which can fairly be presented to it."* (Lord Kelvin).
"There is nothing covered that shall not be revealed" (Luke 12, vss. 2).

ALL over the world, not only in scientific circles, but through the daily press, the attention of thinkers is being drawn to the fact that our old ideas are fundamentally wrong, and that some great truth surely remains undiscovered which is likely soon to bring about a great change for humanity at large.

Lord Kelvin has written: "One word characterises the most strenuous efforts for the advancement of science that I have made perseveringly during fifty-five years—that word is 'failure.' I know no more of electric and magnetic force, or of the relation between ether, electricity, and ponderable matter, or of chemical affinity than I knew and tried to teach my students of natural philosophy in my first session as a professor." This was because Lord Kelvin, whilst a religious man, endeavoured to find truth in matter.

One of the leading and most practical chemists of the day, in mentioning a new discovery which has not yet been given to the world by its learned discoverers, on account of the impossibility of fitting it in with any known theory of matter, made the following statement to me: "It is an extraordinary thing that every science is now coming to a head. This position has been reached before in different sciences, but it is the first time in the known history of the world that all the sciences have come to the same conclusion together, namely, that their old ideas are absolutely wrong." Another, recognised all over the world as a giant in research, said: "We do not know whether we are standing on our heads or on our heels."

The consecutive statement in the following pages contains a collection of facts and logical deductions therefrom, which having been found and demonstrably proved, are gladly presented to suffering humanity. The facts given will, it is believed, be found of fascinating and vital interest to all.

The aim has been, not to present a theory, but first to expose the foundationless fallacies of material so-called laws on which alone rests all this seeming mystery of human experience. Secondly, to draw attention to the only practical, universal, and unfailing method of instantaneously overcoming every kind of sin, disease, and trouble.

*British Association Opening Address.

including death, by a right understanding of Life as God. To understand God is the work of eternity, but a grasp of this method will at once revolutionise the life of the reader. To obtain such a grasp, it is better to read steadily through the sections in the order given, instead of merely taking the most interesting parts first.

THE TRUTHS DECLARED.

The truths declared are not mere arbitrary statements. They can be proved to each and all of those who study the laws herein stated. The main points brought out are as follows:—

1. Sin, disease, and even death itself, are merely crude mistakes, resulting from ignorance of the law of Life, eternal Mind, omnipotent good.
2. God is not a distant potentate, but an ever-living, ever-active, and unalterable Principle—Mind, Soul, Spirit, Life, Truth, and Love; the omnipresence and omnipotence of which can be instantly utilised at any moment and for any good purpose.
3. Man's possibilities, resting on a scientific, mental foundation, are found to be limitless, for he reflects divine Principle. These, even as humanly discerned, are so marvellous that they enable us to form an approximate, and continually improving, conception of absolute spiritual realities.
4. The mysteries of birth and death are explained, the latter being merely a transition into another material state of human consciousness, which can, and very shortly will, be entirely avoided.
5. The changing and fading fallacies with regard to material evolution are laid bare, and the eternal facts of spiritual evolution stated.
6. A logical and consistent statement of the theories of material phenomena, exposing the fallacies that have hitherto, through ignorance, bound mankind, is set forth.

REVOLUTIONARY RESULTS OBTAINABLE.

7. Last, and not least, each reader, as he discerns the truths declared, can at once put into practice himself, an easy, scientific, and therefore infallible and instantaneous method of obtaining the following revolutionary results:—
   (a) Deliverance from sin, disease, and the last grim enemy, death itself.
   (b) Ability to relieve his fellow-man instantaneously of any kind of sin, disease, trouble, and, in fact, help him out of any possible difficulty.
   (c) The overcoming of limitations of all kinds in every right direction.
   (d) Freedom from all worries and troubles, and the attainment of perfect peace of mind, with continued increasing happiness.

" Slumber not in the tents of your fathers; the world is advancing, advance with it" (Mazzini)

Ten years ago I was retained by the "Daily Express" to make a professional examination into mental working, the vital subject that is now engaging the attention of the deepest thinkers and greatest humanitarians throughout the world. In consequence of this I was asked by Mr. Bruce Wallace, under special circumstances, which will be referred to later, to give a lecture, the amplification of which has led to this book.

In the course of the above examination the facts came to my knowledge that are now to be presented to you. These facts, however surprising they may appear to you, were, I assure you, no less so to me. I am convinced, however, that anyone who examines them with even a little care was patience, and with an open mind, will come to the same conclusion as I have done, and reap a rich reward.

I would emphatically echo the words of Uriel to Esdras, who asked for understanding of some of the most important subjects dealt with in this work, and was answered as follows: "The more thou searchest, the more thou shalt marvel" (2, Esdras 4, ver. 26).

"Scepticism is ignorance," writes Victor Longfellow, and a sign of wisdom is to keep our minds open and our mouths shut when scientific wonders are put before us. "Disbelief is easier than belief, if in accordance with environment or custom, and is usually due to indolence, and is never a thing to be proud of" (Romanes).

"Physical research is by far the most important work that is being done in the world" (W. E. Gladstone).

Remember that hardly anything is known scientifically about psychology. It is only recently that it has been deemed worthy of being studied and taught. Professor James, one of the leading psychologists of modern times, writes as follows: "Psychology is but a string of raw facts, a little gossip and a wrangle about opinions, a little classification and generalisation on the mere descriptive level, a strong prejudice that we have states of mind, and that our brain conditions them, but not a single law in the sense in which physics shows us laws. At present psychology is in the condition of physics before Galileo and the laws of motion, or of chemistry before Lavoisier."*

We should be like Sir William Crookes has said, "keep our minds like the windows of a lodging-house, with a notice written thereon, 'Rooms to let.'"

A CORRECT WORD PICTURE.

" And ye shall know the truth, and the truth shall make you free" (John 8, ver. 32).

It is my intention to present, in accordance with the most recent scientific knowledge, a correct word picture; in other words, by the presentation of up-to-date natural science and little-day practical metaphysics, to enable you to understand better what this material world assumes to be, and how through the exposure of all its hidden workings, and therefore seeming mystery, it is possible to emerge from the mists of shifting appearances into the sunlight of eternal facts.

" Psychology," p. 468.

Mr. Balfour, in his presidential address to the British Association a few years ago, pointed out the necessity of not limiting ourselves to material facts alone, but of coming out of the realm of the unreal, that is, the material world, into that which has hitherto been termed abstract, namely, the spiritual world or world of reality.

It is certain that every honest, unprejudiced seeker will find, as I have proved for myself, that the substitution of metaphysical working, or deep systematic thinking, produces practical effects, as far exceeding those obtained by physical methods as sunlight exceeds gaslight.

The theory or explanation of material phenomena, now put before us you has been gradually evolving and includes and accounts for every known so-called fact of the material world, whether physical or so-called mental, accepted by science, or of the class called occult. This theory is daily, although sometimes unknowingly, being corroborated by leaders in natural science all over the world. Many of the most important facts have been confirmed since they were first brought to my knowledge.

F. W. Grant, the author of that most valuable commentary and translation of the Bible known as the "Numerical Bible," which has not yet been generally appreciated, made a special study of the meaning of numbers, which enabled him to obtain great insight into the Bible, and through it into the history of the material world, past, present, and future. Priceless information, essential for the protection of the human race, is recorded in the Bible for the warning, instruction, and consequent immediate safety of those who discern the scientific significance of its spiritual messages. It is interesting to note in connection with the object of this lecture that the same author in his book "Spiritual Law in the Material World," writes as follows: "Standing as I do but at the threshold of all this, or given to enter but a little way, I dare predict to him who shall bring together, as in a stereoscopic picture, the two worlds of Science and Scripture into the unity which they really have, that he shall achieve for himself a joy beyond utterance." This has been the case.

"But all the glories to my arms appealing
I feel no rash raptures win,
As come with majesty and joy of feeling,
From love and light within" (Albert D. Watson).

THE MYSTERIES OF OUR WORLD

"But we speak the wisdom of God in a mystery, even the hidden wisdom, which God ordained before the world unto our glory" (1 Cor. 2, ver. 7.)

Our planet is full of mystery, and of the universe only enough is known to make those who are thought to know a great deal, partially recognise their ignorance. "And if any man think that he knoweth any thing, he knoweth nothing yet as he ought to know" (I. Cor. 8, ver. 2).

Professor Drummond writes: "The one subject upon which all

* To make hypotheses, to verify them by experiments then to attempt to connect, by the aid of generalisation, the facts discovered, represents the stages of progress by the building up of all our knowledge" (Evolution of Matter, p. 317, Dr. Le Bon).

† "Love and the Universe and other Poems."

‡ "Natural Law in the Spiritual World," p. 29.

scientific men are agreed, the one theme upon which all alike become eloquent, the one strain of pathos in all their writing and speaking and thinking, concerns that final uncertainty, that utter blackness of darkness bounding their work on every side." This darkness is ignorance, the mystery of evil, the only cause of the apparent limitation in every direction. This darkness has now been dissipated.

"Occult" Phenomena. Amongst the phenomena known to investigators for which it has hitherto been manifestly impossible to account in any rational way, are those connected with thought-reading, prophesying, clairvoyance, clairaudience, second sight, psychometry, somnambulism, duplicated personality, suggestion, hypnotism, spiritualism, the ancient temples, faith healers, theosophists, the Indian Yogis, Mohammedan fakirs, and the strides and sorcerers of olden days. No instances have as been of such matters that until quite recently their investigation was tabooed by scientific men on the ground that there was no method of obtaining exact knowledge concerning them. There are many other mysterious phenomena, such as ghosts and visions, miracle and enchantments, and marvellous powers that various men have exercised, of which there are many instances recorded in the oldest known writings, in the Bible, and throughout all history. These phenomena are now no longer mysterious, and by reversal of the many fatalities in connection with them they serve as waymarks to better, and ultimately to permanent things, the ideas of God.

Scientific Difficulties. Even if we put on one side all that may be considered "miraculous," those facts which are called "scientific" are just as bewildering. Take, for instance, the ether, which is full of paradoxes. Is a material earth, as stated, flying at the rate of about eighteen miles per second through this ether, the density of which is believed to be 450 times greater than that of the densest matter on the earth? To what are due the deviations in the movements of the Moon and Mercury? Why does the ninth satellite of Saturn revolve in a direction contrary to the others, and contrary to the general rotation of our solar system? Why do the protuberances of the Western hemisphere correspond to the indentations of the Eastern? Why does not the sun get appreciably cooler? Why is a comet attracted, and the particles of its tail apparently repelled, by the sun? Why is the view of so-called natural laws constantly being altered? Why, according to Professor Jevons, can only about one mathematical problem was of a million be solved? Why does chemical affinity work in different ways on different substances? What is electricity? What indeed is vibration or force? What is heat? Why is a bar of steel magnetized under a shock if held in one position and not in another? Why does matter sometimes repel and oftentimes attract water? Why at the temperature of liquid air does phosphorus lose its violent affinity for oxygen and sulphuric acid no longer turn litmus paper red? Why does aluminium, which does not decompose water when cold or oxidise at ordinary temperatures, decompose water violently, and visibly oxidise with water containing the slightest trace of mercury? Why

Sec. I.

do extreme heat and cold produce similar effects? Why does a gyroscope running at a very high speed present a strong resistance to any force used to alter its position? Why does every substance, including water, contract upon cooling, while water and bismuth alone expand just before freezing? What is the cause of the movements of the planets and their satellites? What is gravity? To what are the varying cohesive, elastic, frictional, viscous, electric, and magnetic properties due? What are the laws underlying the freedom and mutual constraints of molecules? Such questions have been puzzling both physicists and chemists for centuries." Nor at last we have the solution.

It is a remarkable thing that the more the materialist has investigated such matters, and the greater his experience of them, the more uncertain has appeared his knowledge and the further he has seemed from any fixed laws. Take, for instance, astronomy. Until recently it was thought the laws governing the movements of the solar system were absolutely fixed and well known. Is it now being found that we had practically no real knowledge of them. Astrologers, who laugh at what they speak of as the ignorance of Western astronomers, will tell you wonderful things that they have learned from applying the facts brought to light by the astronomers, who, confining themselves to the evidence of their five senses, have failed to reap the reward of their discoveries. "Astronomy is the most perfect science, because we know least about it."† (Edward Carpenter.)

All these difficulties can now be demonstrably accounted for by the real metaphysicians, who alone has perfect control over the seeming laws of physics.

Medical Difficulties.—When we come to the subject about which we should know most, namely, man, how little we find is generally known! He is a mass of mystery and contradictions. Take medical practice, for instance. The only certain thing about it is its uncertainty, and yet some of the greatest men have given up their lifetime to its study and almost broken their hearts at different times over their apparent inability to help a sufferer. I've professions have given, and are giving the world up to the present day, such noble examples of self-sacrifice as the medical profession and those connected with it. Yet, in disease lessening! Dr. James Johnson, surgeon to King William IV., said: "I declare my conscientious opinion, founded on long observation and reflection, that if there was not a single physician, surgeon, apothecary, man-midwife, chemist, druggist or drug on the face of the earth, there would be less sickness and less mortality." Why, according to Sir Victor Horsley, do over 10,000 patients die annually in London alone after operations? Why did the Metropolitan Asylums Board recently report in one year alone

† "All the facts of this order (early evolution of matter) belong to the category of unexplained phenomena of which nature is full, and which harness some numerous to show as we point—are most unexplained regions. The complexity of things seems to increase the more they are studied." ("The Evolution of Matter," p 287. Dr. Le Bon)

3 "Modern Science: A Criticism." 39

3,111 cases of mistaken diagnosis admitted to their isolation hospitals. Why did the well-known Dr. Abercrombie write: "Medicine is the science of guessing"? Why does a person apparently die of fright? In fact, when is he really dead, since, as will be shown, he does not really die—that is, pass into another state of consciousness—for several days after the appearance of death? Why does a man's hair turn white in a night—in the case of a Bungalee criminal, in front of the spectators? Why does consciousness almost invariably disappear in moments of danger? Why does one person catch a disease and another under similar circumstances escape it? In fact, what is the cause (so-called) of many diseases? Sir John Forbes, M.D., F.R.S., Fellow of the Royal College of Physicians, said: "No systematic or theoretical classification of diseases or of therapeutic agents ever yet promulgated, is true, or anything like the truth, and none can be adopted as a safe guide in practice." Why is the practice of medicine so different in different countries and at different periods?

Dr. Mason Goode, a well-known Professor, writes: "The effects of medicine on the human system are in the highest degree uncertain; except, indeed, that it has already destroyed more lives than war, pestilence, and famine, all combined." Why did Dr. Benjamin Waterhouse write: "I am sick of learned quackery," and Oliver Wendell Holmes say, in a lecture before the Harvard Medical School: "I firmly believe that if the whole materia medica could be sunk to the bottom of the sea, it would be all the better for mankind and the worse for the fishes"? Why in allopathy is a large amount of a drug given that causes symptoms the opposite of the disease, and in homœopathy a small amount of a drug that produces the same symptoms, and why do both contrary systems produce a seeming cure? One of the latest ideas is to give drugs to increase fevers, on the ground that a fever is nature's method of supplying increased blood to parts affected, so as to get rid of local disease. Why is this so when ice is freely used, and previously the temperature was kept up, both methods producing like results? Why is it that " what is one man's meat is another man's poison"? To what is the effect of infinitesimal homœopathic doses due? Why does a harmless draught surreptitiously substituted for a narcotic mixture equally send a patient to sleep? Why have the drugs used been so constantly changed? In fact, why in civilized countries is the use of drugs being given up altogether? Sir Almroth Wright informs me that "it is useless to expect from the drugs with which we are at present augmented, destruction of the bacteria in the interior of the organism," and that "the method of extinguishing bacteria by the knife will be finally given up." Why are talismans so believed in? What is the explanation of the deaths and cures of sickness produced at a distance by him which doctors in Central Africa, and of the wonderful facts related by thoroughly credible travellers in Siberia, Abyssinia, and elsewhere? Why did the Aïssaoua Arabs, who a little time ago visited London, devour venomous snakes, and allow themselves to be stung by scorpions without harm, after being apparently hypnotised by their chief? To what may the mysterious results be ascribed for which (so)

Healing.—

Physiological Difficulties.—

Unrecognised Human Capacity.—

Unaccountable Animal Wonders.—

100 miles by train? Why do cubs of wild animals, for instance, in moments of danger, obey the dam without a sound being uttered or a movement apparently taking place. How do ants convey to each other a whole series of instructions concerning places to be visited and work to be done, as far as one can tell, by merely momentarily touching each other's antennæ? A scientific friend of mine tells me that, over and over again, he has noticed that if a bird building its nest finds a straw too heavy to lift, it dips one end in water and then is at once able to fly away with it. Why is this? Where does a cat find the fulcrum whereby it falls on its paws even if held only just above the ground with its feet upwards? How is it that a serpent fascinates a bird or frog? Why does a hen remain motionless when it is laid on its back and a line drawn away from its beak? How do soft insects, the smaller death watches, or so-called book lice, make their sounds? How do birds travel for many miles with no apparent movement of their wings?

We now find that the only difference between the material man and material animal is one of degree, and man has unconsciously limited the powers of animals, instead of improving them.

Philosophic Difficulties.—There are also other things of vital importance that have puzzled all thinkers for ages. For instance, why is evil permitted to come into the world? This, amid current times, has been the greatest puzzle to all schools of thought. Why have most of us found ourselves disappointed travellers, aimlessly wandering "on the shores of time," tossed to and fro by adverse circumstances," apparently inevitably subject to sin, disease, and death? Why in this world, on the one hand, is there sometimes, without any apparent reason, such wonderful happiness, though always temporary, while, on the other hand, all nature teems with instances of the most diabolical ferocity and awful misery, making a living hell for countless millions of the seeming lower forms of life, patient, tortured sufferers?

What is the reason of so-called evolution? Is there anything besides Darwin's "natural selection," or, as Wallace puts it, "the struggle for existence"? Huxley spoke of predetermined lines of modification, and since then some biologists, endeavouring to explain evolution, have suggested what they provisionally called Bathmism, i.e., a tendency towards progress inherent in organisms. These and all great thinkers have acknowledged that there must be some further explanation which some day would be discovered.

Finally, why has the world appeared full of mysteries for so long, and why is it that, until recently, the more we learned the more difficulties appeared, and the less we found we really knew?"

"Knowledge is proof that he has learned so much. Wisdom is humble that he knows no more." (Cowper).

The following words of Professor Jevons show our previous lamentable ignorance: "It might be readily shown that in whatever direction we extend our investigations and successfully harmonise

* I feel that Professor S. P. Langley has written: "The more we know, the more we recognise our ignorance; and the more we have a sense of the mystery of the universe and the limitations of our knowledge."

---

a few facts, the result is only to raise up a host of other unexplained facts."

"Even religion and therapeutics need regenerating." No one admits this more fully than the leading exponents of these two great would-be benefactors of mankind.

"At thirty, man suspects himself a fool,
Knows it at forty and reforms his plan;
At fifty chides his infamous delay,
Pushes his prudent purpose to resolve."

We might add that at sixty he regrets his lost opportunities, and at seventy thinks that it is too late to do anything.

One can readily imagine an intelligent, well-informed visitant to this earth for the first time, reporting nearly the whole of its inhabitants to be afflicted with an ignorance of the truth about their own affairs that amounted to insanity.

Such a pitiable state of ignorance does the mass of mankind appear to be in, that we find a well-known writer on astronomy saying: "Science therefore cannot go back to the absolute beginnings of things, or forward to the absolute ends of things. It cannot reason about the way matter and energy came into existence, or how they will cease to exist; it cannot reason about time or space, as such, but only in the relation of them to phenomena that can be observed. . . . Science cannot inquire into them [the facts that are stated in the first chapter of Genesis] for the purpose of checking their accuracy; it must accept them as it accepts the fundamental law that governs its own working, without the possibility of proof" * (E. W. Maunder). This shows something fundamentally wrong in this line of research. Surely we have forgotten the injunction, "Open thou mine eyes, that I may behold wondrous things out of thy law" (Ps. 119, ver. 18).

Dr. J. W. Heysinger has said:—

"What is wanted is to see science put on her spectacles, and get honestly down to hard work on these difficult but universal and most important subjects.

"When that time comes, and it is rapidly coming, psychism, in its broadest sense, will be tried by a jury of its peers, and the verdict will be in accordance with the evidence of all mankind, everywhere and from the beginning, and will not represent merely a self-sufficient ignoring of the whole testimony, and an a priori prejudgment of the whole case. The facts will not be superciliously thrown aside, the evidence will not be perverted nor garbled, inconvenient facts will not be suppressed, the truth will be elicited as it would be by skilled lawyers, and the opinion rendered as it would be by able and impartial judges, and science will then win a crown of imperishable glory. Nay, more, in that day the judgment will be found reflected upon and applicable to many other great problems, now the despair of science, and solid achievements

* "The Astronomy of the Bible," p. 18, 19.

THE MYSTERY OF GOD.

THE SOLUTION OF ALL MYSTERIES.

advanced by Faraday. It should be spoken of as "no-mind" and "non-mental." Human "mind" turns out to be human matter, a mechanical counterfeit of true consciousness, the result of electrical streams in the ether, and therefore, purely ethereal. The only power is Love, alias Mind or God, and we cannot control a matter scientifically by a negative "mind."

The False Spiritual World.—Being utterly ignorant of the ethereal conditions of the final yet elementary state of matter, and knowing that there must be consciousness and therefore reality, mortals have mistakenly conceived of the invisible, ethereal conditions as a spiritual world, and against all logical deductions their buoyant sense of hope has led the majority to think that on death they reach a far-distant "life eternal," as a hypothetical perfect world.

The Real Mind, God.—God, good, is infinite, eternal Mind, and is of necessity eternally good, and good only. Now this is demonstrable. The knowledge of God, heaven, and our real selves is a true mental science, demonstrable through application of the rule of right thinking. So-called "mental" science, which is limited to mere mechanical change of human phenomena, is an entire misnomer, and utterly misleading, and should at best be distinguished as "non-mental" science, because it is not mental and not scientific.

Matter "Non-mental."—Numberless quotations might be given here which show that deep, logical thinkers have recognised that matter cannot possibly be solid fact, but must be merely a form of material impression, false mental, or more accurately, "non-mental," phenomena. The following are instances, and more are given later.

Professor Herbert says: "The common supposition, then, that the material universe and the conscious beings around us are directly and indubitably known, and constitute a world of 'positive' fact, . . . is an entire mistake, based upon astonishing ignorance of the essential limitations of human knowledge."

John Fiske, the well-known historian and professor of philosophy, wrote: "It was long ago shown that all the qualities of matter are what the mind makes them, and have no existence as such, apart from the mind. In the deepest sense, all that we really know is mind, and as Clifford would say, what we call the material universe is simply an imperfect picture in our minds of a real universe of mind-stuff."

Kant also said that "This world's life is only an appearance, a sensuous image of the pure spiritual life and the whole world of sense; only a picture swimming before our present knowing faculty like a dream, and having no reality in itself. For if we should see things and ourselves as they are, we should see ourselves in a world of spiritual natures, with which our entire real relation neither began at birth nor ends with the body's death."

* "The Idea of God," p. 15.

Sec. I.

The practical value to the world of this truth, that was enunciated by many other logical thinkers of equally world-wide reputation, has never been grasped by the majority. Until recently no one has ever followed it up to its logical conclusion, namely, that if the material universe is simply an imperfect false impression, then all that is necessary in order that we should behold the real and perfect universe is to change our thoughts to the standard of perfection, and so see the perfect picture, when the imperfections must disappear and heaven appear.

Matter the Manifestation of false impressions.—" Matter, like space and time, consists in defined."* (W. W. Rouse Ball).

Matter is merely the manifestation of false impression of truth; Lord Kelvin expressed it as "made up of thought forces."† It can be made to appear and disappear by so-called thought, and this in two different ways; one temporary because non-entity, the other disappearance permanent because scientific. Consequently the material world, as long as it has its apparent existence, is subject to continual changes, and has no fixed laws; so-called "thought," literally electric vibration, being the essence of material apparent action. Matter is simply a series of cinematograph pictures.

Carpenter says: "The source of all power is mind."

Professor Huxley says: "If the hypothetical substance of mind is possessed of energy, I for my part am unable to see how it is to be discriminated from the hypothetical substance of matter."

His philosophic position he has summed up as follows: "The key to all philosophy lies in the clear comprehension of Berkeley's problem—which is neither more nor less than one of the shapes of the greatest of all questions, 'What are the limits of our faculties?' And it is worth any amount of trouble to comprehend the exact nature of the argument by which Berkeley arrived at his results, and to know by one's own knowledge the greatest truth which he discovered—that the honest and rigorous following up of the argument which leads us to materialism inevitably carries us beyond it.

The more completely the materialistic position is admitted, the easier it is to show that the idealistic position is unassailable, if the idealist confines himself within the limits of positive knowledge."

And he adds in conclusion: "And therefore if I were obliged to choose between absolute materialism and absolute idealism, I should feel compelled to accept the latter alternative."

Locke, another thinker misunderstood by materialists, writes: "Bodies, by our senses, do not afford us so clear and distinct an idea of active power as we have from reflection on the operations of our minds. Of thinking, body affords us no idea at all. It is only from reflection that we have that. Neither have we from body any idea of the beginning of motion. . . . I judge it not amiss to

* "Mathematical Recreation and Essays," by W. W. Rouse Ball, Fellow and late Tutor of Trinity College, Cambridge.
† I intimate defined matter as a commentary mind, an instantaneous consciousness.

direct our minds to the consideration of God, and spirits, for the clearest idea of active powers . . . God having fitted men with faculties and means to discover, receive, and retain truths, according as they are employed."

A Correct Basic Theory.—*"One scientific theories are perfectly legitimate as long as they are viewed as a means towards practical applications."* (Edward Carpenter).

Hitherto we have tried to fit our facts into our theories, and have had to change our theories so as to explain our new facts. In the correct basic theory now brought to *your* notice, we can fit in our real facts, the facts of good, and the spiritual universe, and at the same time test and account for our so-called facts, which are really only fixed and foundationless beliefs with reference to the material world. In this way we check our knowledge by means of our theory, and prove it later by demonstration. Probed to the bottom, and laid bare, this correct material theory enables us to account rationally for the first time for our so-called facts. We must not, however, dwell on this theory, and build it up in imagination as permanent fact. We have to reverse the illusive truth of this theory, and so give everlasting place to a knowledge of the absolute facts and the spiritual universe. This true knowledge is a revealed and practical science, the science of God as divine Principle, with intelligent, living good as its manifestation.

Every thought a man is conscious of acts to a greater or less extent. Millions now recognise this and are trying to learn how to control illusionary impressions, mis-called thoughts. "Our thoughts are the rudder of our life," says the Rev. I. H. Shannon. Let us then always steer dead straight. "Let the wicked forsake his way, and the unrighteous man his thoughts; and let him return unto the Lord, and he will have mercy upon him" (Is. 55, ver. 7). This is not so easy to do until you know how to do it. It can only be properly done in a scientific way. Let us proceed to advance fearlessly along this way, proving each step as we go.

EVIL AND THE MATERIAL WORLD.

Evil.—*"He that committeth sin is of the devil: for the devil sinneth from the beginning"* (I. John 3, ver. 8).

Everything in the material world is more or less bad or limited. "Christian theology has not been able to make up its mind whether sin is a defect, or a transgression, or a rebellion, or a constitutional hereditary taint, or whether it is all these combined" (W. R. Inge, M.A., D.D., † Professor of Divinity, Cambridge).

Buddhism, which is more of a system of incorrect philosophy than religion as at present taught, teaches that evil is the true kernel

* "The Science of the Future."
† Now Dean of St. Paul's.

---

of existence, only to be removed with the cessation of existence itself. This is true so far as the material world is concerned.

"Our life is a false nature—'tis not in
The harmony of things—this hard decree,
This inexcusable taint of sin" * (Byron).

The Illusion.—*"Before a vigorous inquiry searching, the Reign of Law will prove to be an exploded hypothesis, the uniformity of Nature an ambiguous expression, the certainty of our scientific inferences to a great extent a delusion."* † (Stanley Jevons).

Whence therefore comes this material world, and what is it? The Greeks taught that the nature of sin is delusion or disease—a perverted condition of the mind. Sin, and therefore everything material, everything unlike God, is only delusion, deception, absolute illusion, but not an illusion that the perfect spiritual beings, our true selves, are suffering under, for, being perfect, we could not in reality suffer from any illusion; this exists only as a false claim, an utterly false conception, and this is no true existence. The whole of the material world, with its material phenomena, is as material as mankind's counterfeit of the spiritual realities of all things, and is at best merely a dream, universal illusionary phantasms, a mesmeric sleep, but without even a real dreamer. As Schopenhauer said, it is a distorted dream of humanity. This following illustration may enable you to understand the position better. Hold up your hand between your eyes and a light. Then put a sheet of paper between the hand and eyes, and throw some sand on the paper. Let your hand symbolise the real man, the shadow on the paper the material man, while the sand represents sickness and sin. The shadow on the paper is not the real hand, and if the dirt is rubbed off the paper, then the shadow represents the material man, well and free from sin. Go on rubbing, and the paper will ultimately disappear, and you will see the hand, symbolising the real man.

Again the real man in heaven may be symbolised by a human being in bright sunlight. The shadow then symbolises the material man. As the sun becomes more central the shadow decreases, until ultimately it disappears.

The Devil and Hell.—*The wicked . . . will not seek after God: God is not in all his thoughts"* (Ps. 10, ver. 4).

This material world, this "waste howling wilderness" (Deut. 32, ver. 10), is therefore simply a terrible illusion, a grouping of false impressions, the devil's world, "the very devil," the only devil there is. This "self-imposed agony," this devil or evil, will continue until scientifically disposed of by denying the existence of all wrong thought, and thinking rightly instead. The only devils are the devilish thoughts that attack us. The word "devil" is derived from the Greek "diabolus," which means merely "slanderer." The shadow or that man is material and that there is life in matter. Marianus, writing in the sixteenth century, makes Faustus say to Mephistopheles: "Where are you damned?" Mephistopheles

"Chide Harold," ver. 126. † "Principles of Science," p. 1.
‡ The correct sin, because he is born of God" (I. John 3, ver. 9).
§ Rauhm admits that no true intelligence does not exist in the material world, we have only our extraneous senses to testify to their own existence.
Verily, a costly built upon the sands.
† The word "devil" does not occur in the King James translation of the Old Testament. The only devil there is, is the false concept of being, turned in the Bible, "carnal mind."

replies: "In hell." And so Faustus asking: "How comes it, then,
that thou art out of hell?" he replies: "Why, this is hell, nor am I
out of it."

"Hell hath no limits, nor is circumscribed
In one self place; for where we are is hell,
And where hell is there must we ever be:
And, to conclude, when all the world dissolves,
And every creature shall be purified,
All places shall be hell that are not Heaven."

Heaven and hell are not future states awaiting us at death.
Justin Martyr in 380 A.D. wrote: "If you . . . even dare
blaspheme the God of Abraham . . . and say . . . that the souls,
as soon as they leave the body, are received up into heaven, take
care." " Jesus said: "The kingdom of God is within you" (marg.
ref., "among you") (Luke 17, ver. 21), and we have not to die to
get inside or escape ourselves. "Earth's crammed with heaven"
(Mrs. Barrett Browning). "The fear o' hell's a hangman's whip"
(Burns).

We make our own hell and our own heaven by the way in which
we think, and we have to wake up as fast as we can and get out
of hell—the hell of the wrong thoughts that attack us—into heaven,
a perfect state of consciousness, the world of perfect thoughts,
perfect ideas, the real world that is here round us, if we could
only see it. "Love . . . builds a heaven in hell's despair" (W.
Blake). The only way to escape the suffering which is always
the result of sin is to stop sinning; and the only way to do this
is to stop entertaining wrong thoughts, as will be explained later.
To the mistaken teaching that God made sin, sickness, worries, and
troubles, that is, the material world and material man, is due much
so-called atheism and agnosticism.

"The world is stamped with no more than a footprint of the
Divinity. Its goodness and wisdom are but caricatures of the
Divine, blasphemous because of their very traces of likeness, mimick-
ing the Creator as a marionette mimics its living maker. The
conception of nature as being . . . a direct expression or self-mani-
festation of the Divine character, is responsible for the moral and
spiritual perversions that are everywhere associated with poly-
theistic or pantheistic nature-worship. To worship the caricature
of Divinity there remained to us, is really to worship the devil" †
(Tyrrell).

The Non-reality of Evil and therefore of Matter.—"As for the
other people, which also came of Adam, thou hast said that they are
nothing" (I. Esdras 6, ver. 56). "For if a man think himself to be
something, when he is nothing, he deceiveth himself" (Gal. 6, ver. 3).

The human problem of evil is at length solved. Mathematically
we know that anything that ever was nothing, or ever ceases to exist,

* "Dialogue with Trypho, the Jew" ver. 80.
† "Lex Credit," p. 194.

cannot be real, whatever it may seem to be; therefore evil must be
unreal, however real it may appear, for no logical mind could
believe it to be everlasting. Nothing evil, or even imperfect, can
possibly last, as it is self-destructive. It always disappears sooner
or later. It cannot even harm you when you realise its non-reality.
"They that war against thee shall be as nothing, and as a thing of
nought . . . their works are nothing" (Is. 41, ver. 12, 30).

The non-reality of matter has now been proved. So fixed has
been our belief in its reality that the majority still believe it is
something real and permanent. As this belief changes, so we shall
see a changing world, until the mist of matter disappears, with its
attendant evils, its sickness, worries, troubles, and limitations of every
kind. "The things which are seen are temporal" (II. Cor. 4,
ver. 18).

God, as the Principle of good, is very different from the god
that we have been taught to fear, the god that not only allows but
uses evil to punish the human beings that he is supposed to have
made. How can the Principle of good even know of evil? If God
knows evil He must have known of it beforehand, and therefore
must have intended it, or ordered it, for God, being infinite Mind
and eternal Cause, must necessarily be omniscient and omnipotent.
Habakkuk says: "Thou [God] art of purer eyes than to behold evil,
and canst not look on iniquity" (i. ver. 13). How could
God know of evil and not instantly destroy it? As all sin and
trouble are simply an hypnotic effect, if God could be conscious of
it, "this infinite power would straightway reduce the universe to
chaos." This is one of the proofs of its non-reality, for God is Mind,
and Mind must be all-knowing. "All nations before him are as
nothing; and they are counted to him less than nothing" (Is. 40,
ver. 17). Nebuchadnezzar saw this, and said: "All the inhabitants
of the earth are reputed as nothing" (Dan. 4, ver. 35). "Seeing evil
nowhere exists, for God is all things, and to him no evil is near"
(Origen, about 250 A.D.). All evil is merely a false appearance,
produced by wrong thought. "Its ['the last enemy'] mind and
hostile will, which came not from God, but from itself, are to
be destroyed" (Origen).

"Now the sin of which I speak is this, when a man abandons that
which really exists and serves that which does not really exist, there
is [still] that which really exists, and it is called God" (Melito to
Antonius Caesar, about 160 A.D.).

Jeremiah said: "Out of the mouth of the most High proceedeth
not evil and good?" (Lam. 3, ver. 38), and as John said: "All things
were made by him" (John 1, ver. 3), it is clear that evil is not a
thing, that is, nothing.

In the "Timaeus," Plato depicts the material world as essentially
vile; he is unable to think of the pure and holy Deity as manifested
in it, and accordingly experience this Creator from His creation
[so-called] by the whole breadth of infinity.

* A 16th century Bible, belonging to a friend, translates this—"Canst not see
iniquity; wherefore then lookest"; both translations continue, "upon them
that deal treacherously, and holdest thy tongue when the wicked devoureth
the man that is more righteous than he."

C 2

we read: "I will fear no evil, for thou art with me." This "thou" is God, divine Principle, the law of good, which never fails to destroy the evil if we only think rightly.

Sin the Cause of Disease.—A large proportion of the interminable trouble and myriad forms of disease in this world are acknowledged to be due to sin; perhaps 40 per cent. A medical specialist in diagnosis told me that he thought about 75 per cent. of disease was due either to sin in the individual or sin in his parents. We now find that all disease is due to sin; but in probably sixty out of a hundred cases the sin is the lesser one of what would be popularly called merely wrong thinking, belief in a power other than that of God. This, as will be shown, is the primary cause of all disease and sin. This wrong thinking is due to ignorance.

Socrates said that sin was ignorance. Sin is ignorance of Truth, ignorance of God.

Dr. Thompson, surgeon to H.M. Prisons in Scotland, after observation for eighteen years, says: "I have never seen such an accumulation of morbid appearances as here. Scarcely any die of any one disease, for almost every organ of the body is more or less diseased or degenerated."

The Arraignment of the So-called Man.—"*Man that is born of woman is of few days, and full of trouble. He cometh forth like a flower, and is cut down.... Who can bring a clean thing out of an unclean? not one*" (Job 14, ver. 1, 2, 4).

The five material so-called senses condemn themselves. They cannot see, hear, feel, taste, or smell God. Has God created these "senses" that do not enable us to understand Him in the slightest ! "Theory out of work the body's senses, and thy Divinity shall come to birth" (Secret Sermon on the Mountain in "*Corpus Hermeticum*").

Most people have formed the habit of talking of the human body as something wonderful. It seems to me that it is wonderfully bad. Even a schoolboy could point out many possibilities of improvement. The eye is, I believe, supposed to be the most wonderful part of the human frame. Professor Helmholtz, one of the leading scientific men of modern times, said, referring to the human eye, of which he had made a special study : "Of all our members the eye has always been held as the choicest gift of nature—the most marvellous product." Then, after commenting on its details, he adds: "If an optician would sell me an instrument which had all these defects, I should think myself quite justified in blaming his carelessness in the strongest terms, and giving him back his instrument." If a material man had the different powers of vision apparently possessed in part by the different animals, his sight, although incomparably better than that of human beings, would be quite imperfect in comparison with the power of sight which, as will be soon hereafter, man is capable. The physical eye, however, as will be shown later, is unnecessary for the exercise of this power.

"*Lectures on Scientific Subjects,*" p. 215.

Every other part of man is equally defective," and he does not even rival a lobster, which so easily reproduces a lost limb.

The Ignorant Man a Helpless Victim.—"*Therefore my people are gone into captivity, because they have no knowledge: . . . Therefore hell hath enlarged herself, and opened her mouth without measure*" (Is. 5, ver. 13, 14).

It has been stated that "Man is born free." This is absolutely untrue of the human being. This so-called man is born a helpless babe, and remains helpless, the victim of circumstances, "the football of chance," until he gains some false idea of what God is, and learns how to think rightly. What poor things mortals are, bound together in this bundle of so-called life. Monkeys on a stick, pulled about by conflicting emotions, creatures of impulse, we are swayed by every passing thought whilst we are learning how to control these thoughts. This lamentable position can only continue until man knows how to think rightly, and thus exercises his rightful dominion.

The Death Struggle of Nature.—"*For the earnest expectation of the creature waiteth for the manifestation of the sons of God. . . . For we know that the whole creation groaneth and travaileth in pain together until now*" (Rom. 8, ver. 19, 22).

Darwin showed the fierce struggle that lies beneath the seeming peace of nature. Many sensitive natures have been overwhelmed, and are daily being overwhelmed, by this universal unrelenting nature, "red in tooth and claw."

Dr. Macpherson, of Edinburgh, says that "a mere segment of an eternity will fight with a segment of an Australian ant, under the unmistakable influence of rage, until exhaustion or death ensues." Even with the smaller animal life one sees this. Romanes, in "Animal Intelligence," gives particulars of a conflict between a small rodent and a larger one, and Sir William Dawson states that "an amoeba shows volition, appetite, and passion." The pious Jacobi is stated to have said: "Nature conceals God; man reveals God." Haeckel writes: "The raging war of interests in human society is only a feeble picture of the unceasing and terrible war of existence which reigns throughout the whole of the living world."

Many of these present must have felt the oppressive sense, referred to in the words :—

"My soul is sick with every day's report
Of wrong and outrage with which earth is filled " ?
(Wordsworth).

No wonder Philip Mauro, who speaks of this world-system as "stupendous, gigantic, remorseless, terrifying !" says: "Though

* The report of Sir George Newman, the Chief Medical Officer of the Board of Education, shows that out of some 6,000 odd children examined, 62 per cent. were diseased, of which 13 per cent. had serious defective vision, and 70 per cent. extensively decayed teeth.

† "Confession of Faith," p. 73.

‡ "The Patriot."

composed apparently of human beings, and existing presumably for human beings, it nevertheless devours men, women, and children, placidly, and for trifling considerations.

Goethe, with all his prosperity and riches, states that he had not had five weeks of genuine pleasure in his whole life; and Caliph Abdul-rahman said that in fifty years he had had only fourteen days of pure happiness. Many have not had that small amount. How different it is when one knows how to think rightly.

Fiske, the well-known historian, says: "In every part of the animal world we find implements of torture surpassing in devilish ingenuity anything that was ever seen in the dungeons of the Inquisition. We are introduced to a scene of incessant and universal strife, of which it is not apparent on the surface that the outcome is the good or the happiness of anything that is sentient."

"If the Creator of such a world is omnipotent, He cannot be actuated solely by a desire for the welfare of His creatures, but must have other ends in view to which this is in some measure subordinated. Or if He is absolutely benevolent, then He cannot be omnipotent, but there is something in the nature of things which sets limits to His creative power."*

On the other hand, with the lowest there is a sense of good. A friend of mine recently heard a miserable, poverty-stricken wretch, slouching along in the cold, soliloquising as follows: "Gawd 'elp the poor wretches as 'ave no 'ome of their own this weather." Few of us are thankful enough for what we have.

Wonders of the World.—Most people are ignorant of the immensity and diversity of the universe, or else they could not possibly have thought of God as they have done. Our solar system, which itself appears to be rushing through space at about twelve miles per second—the velocity of one star is 200 miles a second—is a mere speck in the heavens, and yet the orbit of Neptune, the farthest planet of the system is, on an average, 2,791 millions of miles from the sun. A train running at sixty miles an hour would take over 3,700 years, nearly the whole of historical time, to traverse the distance. Alpha, in Centaur, the nearest fixed star in the sky, is about 25 millions of millions of miles from it, yet the great Nebula in Orion has been stated to be 200 times the distance from the sun of the nearest fixed star. The speed of light would enable it to travel round the equator seven times in a second; yet it would travel round 1,000 million times during the four and one-third years it takes to come from Alpha Centauri. The number of the stars perceptible by means of the great telescopes is estimated at 400 millions, red, orange, yellow, green, blue, purple, etc. Over 100 million stars are now capable of being photographed. Many of these are of an enormous size; for instance, Rigel in Orion and Betelgeux in the same, are at an immeasurable distance away, and must exceed our sun many thousands of times in volume, in mass,

* "The Idea of God."

and in splendour. The great northern sun, Canopus in Argo, is estimated by Carl Snyder as having a volume more than 1,000,000 times that of our sun.

"The sum of the universe ... is quite appalling when we comprehend it, for it seems really to be infinite, to have no boundary. Space and the worlds in space—numbered worlds, many of them, no doubt—extend beyond the reach of the largest telescope." (Sir Oliver Lodge, D.Sc., LL.D., F.R.S.)

Robert Blatchford, in "God and My Neighbour," writes as follows: "On earth there are forms of life so minute that millions of them exist in a drop of water. There are microscopic creatures more beautiful and more highly finished than any gem, and more complex and effective than the costliest machine of human contrivance. In 'The Start of Creation,' Mr. Edward Clodd tells us that one cubic inch of rotten stone contains 41,000 million vegetable skeletons of diatoms.

"Talk about Aladdin's palace, Sinbad's valley of diamonds, Macbeth's witches, or the Irish fairies! How petty are their exploits, how tawdry are their splendours, how paltry are their riches, when compared to the romance of science.

"Do you believe that the God who imagined and created such a universe could be petty, base, cruel, revengeful, and capable of error? I do not believe it."

The Arraignment of the So-called God.—The national attitude of ignorance regarding God in the past is shown by the phrase in legal contracts referring to unavoidable disasters as "acts of God." Even so-called civilisation has its devilish side. According to Victor Lougheed, in the United States 12,000 people are annually killed and 70,000 injured by railway traffic.

Baxter, the religious writer, actually states that God Himself will take infinite pleasure in the eternal torments of the damned.* The Rev. M. Baxter told me that we should literally see all the scenes depicted in the Apocalypse.

The lie that God made matter, this mist that hides from us the real and glorious spiritual world, has brought forth such statements as the following: "It is His world, remember. He made it, and He is omnipotent ... why did not He make it better? If it is wayward and intractable, it can be no more than He expected, or ought to have expected. Whereas consists His right to punish us for our transgressions? Suppose we challenge it; what will He say in defence?" Benson writes: "The essence of God's omnipotence is that both law and matter are first and originate from Him; so that if a single fibre of what we knew to be evil can be found in the world, either God is responsible for that, or He is dealing with something He did not originate and cannot overcome. Nothing can extricate us from this dilemma, except that what we think evil is not really evil at all, but hidden good." This is obviously impossible. Under no circumstances can evil be good, and it can never be less nor more than evil; but it has only recently

* Mr. C. H. Enock in a recent paper read before the Institution of Electrical Engineers, stated that in 1907 no less than 134,651 people were killed or injured in Britain and the United States.

* "Spiritual Everlasting Rest," chap. 6.

‡ The Rev. R. H. Benson in a paper against Christian Science read at the Roman Catholic Conference at Brighton, 1908, said: "that we may show ... how supposedly on the very doctrine of the spiritual stock that God has built around to heaven, hangs the doctrine of the Incarnation, by which the Creator became linked indelibly to the creature, and the spiritual to the material, in bonds that are eternal." This is practically pantheism.

been discovered that evil, as manifested illusion, will temporarily hide from us the permanent good, until this good is understood and acknowledged to be spiritual, tangible, the only reality.

Could a God of even the human standard of morality have made this material evil world of rampant injustice, or could such a hellish wilderness of tangled dreams form part of an original perfect conception? Read Mr. William Watson's arraignment of the Powers of Europe at the time of the Armenian massacres, and then think:—

"Yes, if ye could not, though ye would, lift hand—
Ye halting leaders—to abridge Hell's reign.
If such your plight, most hapless ye of men!
But, if ye could, and would not, oh, what plea
Think ye shall stand you at your trial, when
The thunderclowd of witnesses shall loom
At the Assizes of Eternity!"

Haeckel truly writes: "If the one God is really the absolutely good perfect Being they proclaim, then the world which He has created must also be perfect. An organic world so imperfect and full of sorrow as exists on this earth He could not possibly have conceived."

Now God is the greatest friend and guide that a man can have, a very present help in every kind of trouble. Poor, deluded humanity! What a horrible penalty it pays for ignorance of God. How fatally it is deceived.

Good.—"Mercury is [goodness] seeketh not to enter into the soul, for it is there already, only it is unperceived" ("Theologia Germanica").

God, the Principle of good, never made the material world, nor even could have made, or even knew of, such a horrible nightmare. If so He is unquestionably responsible. Sin, disease, and death are absolutely unnatural. The true God made the real world, and we find the Bible statement scientifically accurate: "And God saw everything that he had made, and, behold, it was very good" (Gen. 1, ver. 31). The material world is only a false sense of the real or spiritual world, which is here now and everywhere, and which, to those who look for it, shines through the visible world in glimpses of eternal verities. "I expect that the great mass of the beauty around us is hidden from us, even from us the highest at present" (Sir Oliver Lodge, F.R.S.).

"For so the whole round earth is every way
Bound by gold chains about the feet of God"
(Tennyson).

The material world is fortunately not a fact. It is only a series of illusionary false beliefs about the real world which is here around us if we could only perceive it and be conscious only of perfection. "Men ... changed the truth of God into a lie" (Rom. 1, ver. 25). "Other world! There is no other world. God is one and omnipresent: here or nowhere is the whole fact" (Emerson).

"Theism ... recognises an Omnipresent Energy, which is none other than the living God. The presence of God is the one all-pervading fact of life, from which there is no escape" (John Fiske). Consequently, the love, the life, the beauty, the joy, the wisdom, "radiant realities of God's creation," in fact, all the good of which we, unfortunately, only get indications in this so-called material world, is real, made by God. "Lo, this only have I found, that God hath made man upright; but they have sought out many inventions" (Eccles. 7, ver. 29). The man that God made is perfect, sinless, and eternal. Paul said: "Neither death, nor life ... nor things present, nor things to come, nor height, nor depth, nor any other creature, shall be able to separate us from the love of God." He knew well enough that the real man was part of the Christ, and never could be separated from God, divine Love. "The earth is full of the goodness of the Lord" (Ps. 33, ver. 5). This is spoken of the permanent and perfect, spiritual earth.

Matter, while held in its place by ignorance and false belief, merely hides from us the real spiritual earth, with all its spiritual beauty and goodness, so that we get a limited, material sense of it, instead of seeing it as it really is. How fortunate is it that we get even glimpses of reality, intuitional, significant, timely foreshadowings of the truth.

"O world that God has made it! All is beauty; and knowing this is love, and love is duty"! (Robert Browning).

Sir Oliver Lodge says: "Everything sufficiently valuable, be it beauty, artistic achievement, knowledge, unselfish affection, may be thought of as enduring henceforth and for ever ... as part of the eternal Being of God."

"And all that is at all,
Lasts ever, past recall;
Earth changes, but thy soul and God stand sure"
(Robert Browning).

EVOLUTION OF OUR SENSE OF GOD.

"Every human institution, therefore, religion itself, in for so time can affect it—is exposed to inevitable decay. Accordingly, a religion which is not working for a revival is making any till it be swept away. Christianity has always reformed itself, and will to the end of time continue to reform itself, by going back to the words and to the life of Christ"; (Max Müller).

When mortal so-called man was a mere brute beast he had no God; he did not even understand what good was, and probably ate his children if he could get at them. This stage of ignorance is alluded to in the second verse of the first chapter of Genesis as "darkness." This first chapter can be looked upon as a symbolic description of the real or spiritual world, referred to by John in chap. 1, ver. 3, of his Gospel, when he said, "All things were made by him." The

The Religion of Many Gods.—" *God forbid that we should forsake the Lord, to serve other gods*" (Josh. 24, ver. 16).

IS THE REAL MAN MATERIAL OR SPIRITUAL?

MAN IS NOT MATERIAL.

The Material or Carnal Man as Described in the Bible.

now thyself with him, and be at peace: thereby good shall come unto thee" (Job 22, ver. 21). "And this is life eternal, that they might know thee the only true God" (John 17, ver. 3). We have to gain a true conception of God and man, the divine man. In proportion as we gain a better understanding of the "spotless selfhood" of God, so do we become more like Him, and more like our real selves, which are created "in the image of God," good, and "in the likeness of God" (Gen. 1, ver. 27, and 9, ver. 1). The acknowledgment of the perfection of the one, infinite God, and the realisation that God is All "confers a power withing else can." The Ego is God: infinite Soul. Man is the reflection of the Ego, consistent with God, being the eternally divine idea. God is infinite individuality, one living Principle, for God is Life and God is All. Can one say more?

"All is of God that is and is to be,
And God is good, let this suffice us still!"

(Whittier).

The beginner, in his path upwards, may at one time think that he has lost his God, when he recognises that God is Principle; but soon after he will joyfully admit that he has found the Christ, Truth: Life, Truth, and Love. (See Note F on page 503.)

Browning makes Paracelsus say: "By intuition positive knows: and I knew at once what God is, what we are, what life is. Alas! I could not see the knowledge aright? Now we can use this knowledge, which, as a lens, magnifies the divine powers that are a present possibility to all, until so recognised that we use them to the full extent, for the benefit of all mankind. What a glorious life then appears before us, enabling us to step out into the sunlight of Truth. "God-crowned."

"What we require is no new Revelation, but simply an adequate conception of the true essence of Christianity" ("Paradoxical Philosophy").

Wisdom.—"Knowledge practically applied to the best ends" ("New Century Reference Library Dictionary").

To know Truth we require wisdom. Solomon gives us a scientifically accurate statement of man's inherent ability to attain to true knowledge. He says: "He hath given me certain knowledge of the things that are, namely, to know how the world was made, and the operation of the elements: The beginning, ending, and midst of the times ... And all such things as are either secret or manifest, them I know. For wisdom, which is the worker of all things, taught me; for in her is an understanding spirit, holy, one only, manifold, subtil, lively, clear, undefiled, plain, not subject to hurt ... She is the breath of the power of God, and a pure influence flowing from the glory of the Almighty ... I preferred that I should not otherwise obtain her, except God gave me her; and that was a point of wisdom also to know whose gift she was: I prayed unto the Lord, and besought him" (Wisdom of Solomon 7, ver. 17, 18, 21, 22, 24, and 8, ver. 7).

"Though thou invest the earthly Wisdom now, yet when thou shalt be united now with the Heavenly Wisdom, then thou wilt see that all the Wisdom of the World is Folly; and wilt see also

that the World hates not so much thee, as thine Enemy, which is the Mortal Life" (Jacob Boehme). This mortal life is now found to be merely a mistaken, and therefore false, view of life.

Theology.—"The science that treats of the existence, nature, and attributes of God, especially of man's relations to God" ("New Century Reference Library Dictionary").

Of the three classes of thinkers endeavouring to ascertain truth, referred to earlier, let us take first the theologian, as his work is the endeavour to gain and teach the knowledge of God. Whether Truth passes under the theologian's name of God, Elohim, or Jehovah, under the scientific man's name of cause or nature, or under the metaphysician's name of Mind, we find that religion, which we may almost define as the endeavour to understand and practise the law of God, or good, has, taken as a whole, presented a steady evolution. Such an idea, for instance, as eternal punishment, or "aimless torture, and eternal roasting amidst noxious vapours," as it has been described, is now almost given up by the more spiritual and cultured classes. The idea of atonement is now altering. No longer does a view of God as a jealous, one may almost say a savage God, sacrificing his dearly beloved Son, appeal to us.

Absolute good or Truth is the Mind that includes all life, truth, love, wisdom, and joy, in fact, all the good. The statement that God cannot know evil, and therefore cannot know the material world, existed as much hostility ten years ago as the assertion of universal salvation did fifty years ago, when men thought that salvation was their reward for being as good as they could be, not recognising that material thought is the instrument of all reward or punishment in a material world. "Behold, the righteous shall be recompensed in the earth: much more the wicked and the sinner" (Prov. 11, ver. 31).

To think that God can know evil is equal to saying that eternal consciousness of infinite goodness can at the same time be conscious of evil, an obvious impossibility, even for a moment, as it is equivalent to saying that black is white.

So many have been the hopeless inconsistencies in the material world, that we have quite calmly fallen into the habit of accepting as true such absolutely illogical statements.

Soon there will be no further cause for Carlyle's scathing remarks: "Quackery and dupery do abound in religion; above all, in the more advanced decaying stages of religion they have fearfully abounded; but quackery was never the originating influence in such things; it was not the health and life of religion, but their disease, the sure precursor that they were about to die."

The only real test of a religion is: Are its doctrines demonstrable? "The only perfect religion is divine Science, Christianity as taught ...

* The Supernatural Life.

Sec. I.

Even Philosophy has its paralyzing dogma. The celebrated Auguste Comte actually proposed the creation of a committee to limit the scientific researches which should be permitted.

Both scientific and religious dogma is fast fading. Dr. Campbell Morgan, possibly the most "orthodox" Evangelical among leading Congregational ministers, said recently in one of his sermons, "Ten years ago, when I began my ministry (aged 30) in this pulpit, there were things in theology upon which I would have dogmatised as I cannot dogmatise now."

The Three Stages of Truth.

Professor Agassiz says: "Every great scientific truth goes through three stages. First, people say it conflicts with the Bible. Next, they say it has been discovered before. Lastly, they say they had always believed it." T. J. Hudson amplifies this, and says: "First, it is met by a universal shout of derision. When that fails to discover it, as it sometimes does, everybody claims it as his own. When that is disproved, as it sometimes is, each claimant proceeds to prove himself with a deal of old libraries as an effort to prove that it was always known."

Indifference, as Lawrence Wetherell says, is a "robber of opportunities," and I am not sure that it does not keep a man back more than aggressive suspicion.

New Truths are Hateful to the Sluggard.

A Baptist Minister of Arkansas is said to have told some members of his congregation, on his return from a summer visit to Fort Smith, that he had seen men running on a foot track. The congregation, who were "sound orthodox believers," received this statement with amazement, being doubtful whether he was not mad. The giant intellect of the deacons quickly settled the question, for, "As the Lord could not make men more than three and a half inches thick in that country, in the winter, to say that a man could make of a foot track in the summer was a lie so contrary to reason and experience as to be preposterous," and thus the preaching was turned out of the church for his scandalous lying.

H. Croft Hiller in "Hercules," writes: "New truths are hateful to the gnathic-thy public of science included. All is a case of struggling in familiar mud-holes. Science will have nothing to do with so-called occultism and truths metaphysical because the truths of occultism and metaphysics are not in the parish of science."

Throughout the world the exponents of physical science have been held up to mankind as matters ridicule by those familiar with occult matters now recognised as merely having to do with shifting forces, ethereal phenomenon. Many of the truths now put forward although new to the natural scientist, or only recently admitted, have been, as a matter of fact, known and taught for years. Fortunately, this habit of burying our heads in the sand has now passed, and all workers are on the look out for the higher truths. "Strive for the truth unto death, and the Lord shall fight for thee" (Ecclus. 4, ver. 28).

At the same time, as Huxley has said, "Take nothing for truth without once knowing that it is such."

"Scripture at last saw we are shand."

"Mrs. Eddy, forty years ago, gave the world the details of what is now beginning to be accepted as the correct explanation of the universe. Dr. Olcott, lecturing on April past, said, at the Pembridge's Hall, Madras, so much she followed statement ... Electricity cannot accept under prepared conditions, he sees; yet it is matter. The universal order of science on the ether now; yet it is matter in a class of universe tenuity." This now comes not to be correct.

Sec. I.

51

W. M. Salter says: "The Mighty Power hid from our gaze by the thin screen of nature and of nature's laws . . . is with our struggles after a perfect right." "If God be for us, who can be against us?" (Rom. 8, ver. 31).

Philosophy.—"The knowledge of the causes of the phenomena both of mind and matter" ("New Century Reference Library Dictionary").

Philosophy, like a moth fluttering round an incandescent electric lamp, has, as will be shown hereafter, continually touched the fringe of the truth, that truth Plato so desired to know. Sankaracharya, a noble representative of Hindu thought, taught that perfect knowledge was perfect bliss. Knowledge of God is eternal life, and at last Philosophy is on the threshold of truth, with the door open wide, very wide, to the glorious light now shining.

The great merit of such men as Descartes is that they are open-minded enough to view as doubtful what up to their time had been considered uncontested truths. We all have to maintain this position, which is really the outcome of logical reasoning. As Dr. Le Bon says: "Too often do we forget that the scientific idols of the present day have no more right to invulnerability than those of the past." Truth must be demonstrably true.

Science.—"Knowledge, the comprehension of truth or facts; truth ascertained" (Webster).

"If the time is ever to come in the religious history of the human race when what may be called God's Science of Man is to supersede theology, which is man's Science of God, that time is already here" (J. W. Heysinger, M.D.). At last we begin to understand the Science of Mind.

Science, "the atmosphere of God," is eternal, and includes all truth. Natural science, like theology, has also been hampered by its dogma. Dr. Heysinger writes: "The dogmatism of theology and such a full counterpart and co-worker in her newer sister, dogmatic science. The scientific pursuit is a noble one to espouse, the work is grand beyond comparison, the fruits are already priceless and vast; but specialities always narrow the field of vision of the specialist, and the time for dogmatism has not yet come, and will not come for ages, if at all."

Writing of the extraordinary phenomenon that natural scientists are now admitting must point to some great underlying facts of life, he also says: "I do not fully understand these things, but that is no reason why I should allow others, who understand them very much less, or not at all, to do the understanding for me. I agree with Professor De Morgan that . . . the physical explanations I have seen are easy, but miserably insufficient . . . I merely

* "The Revolution of Forces."
† "Spirit and Matter before the Bar of Modern Science."
‡ "Scientific ideas which rule the minds of scholars at various epochs have all the solidity of religious dogmas" (Dr. Le Bon).

every hand for another echo of the Voice of which Revelation also is the echo, that out of the mouths of two witnesses its truths should be established . . . Science . . . speaks to Religion with twofold purpose. In the first place, it offers to corroborate Theology in the reward, by purify it. If the removal of suspicion from Theology is of urgent moment, not less important is the removal of its adulterations . . . the artificial accumulations of centuries of uncontrolled speculation . . . they mark the impossibility of progress without the guiding and sustaining hand of Law.

We are in the midst of a mental revolution. Sir Oliver Lodge has written: "The region of religion and a complete Science are one." This complete knowledge, "the seal of Deity" having "the impress of heaven," is divine, and is now at hand. For years science has been separating itself from the fatalities of religion, and the greatest theologies of the twentieth century have been slowly divorcing themselves from it. Now the light has come, and again the two are wedded together, this time with an indissoluble bond, the hand of the knowledge of truth. "Science is surely moving in the direction of the spiritual; nothing can be more certain." * (J. W. Reynolds, M.D.) Many of nobler, science would endeavour to give the meaning of Spirit.

Ethics. — *The science that treats of the principles of human morality and duty*" ("New Century Reference Library Dictionary").

"Ethical Science is already for ever completed, so far as her general outline and main principles are concerned, and has been, as it were, waiting for physical science to come up with her" ("Paradoxical Philosophy"). Physical science has now come up.

The World's Awakening. — *Religion is a great reality and a great truth—nothing less than an essential and indestructible element of human nature* (Herbert Spencer).

True religion is helping our fellow-men. For this it is necessary to obtain a better knowledge of God. The world is fast waking up to the true knowledge of God and all that this means. We are seeing that we cannot be pushed into heaven at the last moment by a blind belief in an immense sacrifice of a dearly-beloved Son, but that we receive, day by day, moment by moment, only the results of the right and wrong thinking of ourselves and others. Fortunately, we are now recognising that by right thinking we rise into a consciousness of complete dominion over the evil that hitherto may have appeared irresistible. "For since by man came death, by man came also the resurrection" (I. Cor. 15, ver. 21). "Blessed and holy is he that hath part in the first resurrection" (Rev. 20, ver. 6). The Greek word, "Anastasis," translated resurrection, means primarily, "an *awaking* from sleep."

"Come now, and let us reason together, saith the Lord" (Is. 1, ver. 18). For the first time in the world's history every man's highest reasoning faculty can be satisfied by the demonstrable truth that is now flooding the world, proving beyond all doubt the omni-

* * Spirit and Matter before the Bar of Modern Science," p. 308.

potence of good, at all times, and under all circumstances. "Awake thou that sleepest, and arise from the dead, and Christ shall give thee light" (Eph. 5, ver. 14). "The entrance of thy words giveth light" (Ps. 119, ver. 130). "The true Light which lighteth every man that cometh into the world" (John 1, ver. 9). This is the light of the knowledge of God and His manifestation, heaven.

WHAT IS HEAVEN?

"*Eye hath not seen, nor ear heard, neither have entered into the heart of man, the things which God hath prepared for them that love him. But God hath revealed them unto us by his Spirit*" (I. Cor. 2, ver. 9, 10.)

The material, sensuous man, gradually waking up, progressing towards a better recognition of the real and therefore spiritual existence, finds out that heaven is "not a local habitation, but the harmony of mind and body," a perfect state of consciousness in which his real self exists at the present time. He also finds that this sense of a material world, including his apparent selfhood, is only a false sense which, when corrected by the true knowledge of God, disappears." That is to say, the human being gradually loses a false sense of the world as material, and appears ultimately to see things as they really are, passing through the gate of truth into "the heaven of Soul." The human body and so-called "mind" will, we must, be ultimately entirely dematerialised, for "flesh and blood cannot inherit the kingdom of God; neither doth corruption inherit incorruption" (I. Cor. 15, ver. 50). Then it will be universally demonstrated that man has never actually existed in a material body or been dependent upon such an imperfect organisation. "That which is born of flesh is flesh, and that which is born of the Spirit is spirit." (John 3, ver. 6).

The Kingdom of God that is Within. — *It is given unto you to know the mysteries of the kingdom of heaven*" (Matt. 13, ver. 11).

The following statements with regard to heavenly realities are neither speculative nor arbitrary, but logical conclusions, drawn from scientific premises, and proved by demonstrations over limitations of material laws.

"Heaven is not," a noted preacher once said in a sermon, "an eternal sitting in damp clouds, playing on harps, and singing praises to God, as so many seem to think."

It has recently been recognised that we make our own hell and our own heaven here, and few men are fiends enough to want a worse hell for anyone than many men are temporarily in at the present moment, the hell of their own wrong thoughts, due to their not knowing how to think rightly. "The mind is its own place, and

* * Ever pointed out that the material world was wholly different from the real, and that by the action of our minds we could never know its true. This is true of all the material man, but not once of the real man, who is spiritual.

Sec. I.

reflecting God's ideas, expressing our ideals in new creations or groupings. This redistribution of God's thoughts is the source of infinite happiness, individual and universal.

Happiness can be differentiated into four principal divisions:—
First, every spiritual being loves his fellow-man, even the one for the first time, with a love of which the material man can hardly form even a faint conception, because it is the perfect love of God.

Secondly, we are always interchanging perfect ideas with those we love, either individually or otherwise.

Thirdly, we are continually manifesting God's power of grouping together new combinations of glorious ideas, so giving our fellow-men fresh happiness, and consequently gaining the highest happiness ourselves.

Fourthly, we can awaken with those we love amongst infinite worlds of unthinkable beauty.

These four chief sources of real happiness are counterfeited by four in the material world. First, we have the love towards our fellow-man; secondly, the interchanging of ideas with those we love; thirdly, even the making of a rag doll for a child gives us a sense of happiness that would no follow many a greater action prompted by a lesser motive; and, fourthly, who has not been lifted heavenwards by the beauty and grandeur lying behind Nature's handiwork?

The reason for this is, that all the love and happiness of which we get only glimpses in this material world are real, though limited.

> Souls that are gentle and still
> Hear the first music of this
> Far off, infinite bliss" (Sir Edwin Arnold).

Reality of Good.

Now all that this material world indicates of good is real; the love, the life, the beauty, the joy, etc. We get at times glorious glimpses of this reality through the mist; wonderful love, marvellous beauty, unspeakable joy. "For now we see through a glass darkly" [1 Cor. xi, ver. 12], and "through every grass-blade the glory of the present God still beams" (Carlyle).

Earth's crammed with heaven and every bush afire with God," another has said. As we progress, the mist gets thinner, and with this advancement dawns a foretaste of God's world. To limit future good is unquestionably to limit God. Matter, apparently hiding the existence of the spiritual realities, only hides their perfection from us, giving us a false sense of the real itself, and as the matter is dematerialised the glorious realities of these perfect ideas gradually appear clearer and clearer.

"The ideal is the real, well seen" (Carlyle). "The realities of existence can be conceived, and they are probably assailing us, stimulating and guiding us in ways of which we are only half conscious, and some of us are conscious at all" (Sir Oliver Lodge, D.Sc., LL.D., F.R.S.).

> "A thing of beauty is a joy forever;
> Its loveliness increases, it will never
> Pass into nothingness" (Keats).

Pope little knew the depth that lay behind his words "One truth is clear, whatever is, is Right."

Sec. I.

Proof of Our Knowledge of Heaven.

The way to prove whether or not your knowledge of heaven is true is this: If anything is going wrong in the material world, and you realise clearly enough the spiritual perfection of the reality, of which that "wrong" is the counterfeit, the instantaneous disappearance of the trouble will indicate your realisation to have been correct. This means that the difficulty in the material world is immediately put right. This is one important difference between true knowledge and that put forward by the various schools of religious thought; namely, that you are now able to prove your theory by direct experiment, and have not to rely solely upon logical deduction.

Another important difference is that, if the mental called "you" is thinking scientifically, realising constantly that you—your real spiritual, not material "you"—are led by God, then, through the action of God in destroying evil, the mental "you" appears to be led by God, the Principle of good, just as the way that a young child is taught and pretended by its mother when learning first to walk.

Movement Instantaneous. — All stars and mountain peaks are thought of the Eternal Mind (Parmenides).

Movement Instantaneous.

of, and shares with his fellow-man, all the bounties that are delighting him, to an infinitely greater degree than the human being does when in the midst of beautiful surroundings.

When the enjoyment has been obtained from being conscious of these lovely ideas, the other spiritual being, desirous of returning the happiness that he has received, and being reminded of past enjoyment of heavenly bounties, can draw the attention of his fellow-man to the spiritual reality of some ideas in another planet, say Jupiter. All that is necessary, then, is to think of these ideas, and at once they are both conscious of the new ideas connected with the spiritual reality of Jupiter.

Practical Results an Undeniable Proof.—"*Let us not regret experience on the ground of dogmatic assertion and heedless speculation.*"[*] (Sir Oliver Lodge, D.Sc., LL.D., F.R.S.)

The proof of the above being true is found through its practical application. If in the material world you find that you have lost your train or apparently have not time to go from one place to another, you can get over the difficulty by turning in thought to God, denying the reality of the trouble and realizing that in heaven man goes instantly from one idea to another, or you can realize that man is always in the right place. Then, through this reversal of thought and your recognition of the action of God as taking place in heaven, the wrong ethereal thoughts that appear as forms of trouble are destroyed, and you find yourself out of the difficulty, although you cannot be certain that what usually happens will occur. For instance, sometimes you will find on going to the station that there is another train that you knew nothing about, sometimes that a ship could has been put on to a later express, or the difficulty disappears in some other way. Sometimes the unrecognized action of God results in your finding that there has been no need to go at all, and that the object of your going has been effected in some unexpected way.

Perfect Sequence of Thought.—In heaven an individual called, never can be caused some, but is always exactly the thing most desirable, as there is always a perfect sequence of thought, and the two, with mutual rejoicings blend in true unity of joint appreciation of the wonderful ideas of God. To indicate the perfect sequence of thought it may be stated that when you have finished listening to, for instance, a glorious sonata—we have to use material expressions—and are called to admire a beautiful piece of scenery, this scenery is an exact visual (we must again, unfortunately, use a

---

material expression, representation, of the sonata," and a further unfoldment of perfection. Whatever one does, it brings infinite happiness to all concerned. In this material world we move with trouble and even danger from one place to another, and often, whilst thinking of something totally inconsequent, politely cover a pawn with our hand whilst our neighbour points out what he thinks the beauties of nature.

Spiritual Reality of Parts of the Body.—
"*What if earth,
Be but the shadow of heaven, and things therein
Each to each other like, more than on earth is thought.*" (Milton.)

Everything in the material world only counterfeits and finds the existence of spiritual reality. For instance, the spiritual reality of the hand is the power to grasp an idea. The reality of the teeth is the capacity to analyse and dissect the idea; your material digestive organs counterfeit the power with which you digest, assimilate, and understand the ideas, and the arm counterfeits the power with which, in the reality, you reflect them, that is, call the attention of your fellow-man to them, or pass them on. The spiritual reality of the lower limbs is the power to move in thought from idea to idea. That is, as mentioned, you can call the attention of your fellow-man to lovely ideas, even the spiritual reality of any planet or star, and directly you think of them you have all the effect of being there and enjoying them together.

Man being made in the image and likeness of God, every aspect of God has its reflection in him. Consequently, the reflection of every synonym is counterfeited by some portion of the material man.

There are three great synonyms of God—Life, Truth, and Love. So, there are three important organs in man which counterfeit the real organs of the spiritual man. The real spiritual lungs are the reflection of God as Life, through which man receives the ideas of God; the liver, the reflection of God as Truth, through which man arranges the ideas, and groups them together into new combinations, to be reflected to his fellow-man; the heart, the reflection of God as Love, through which the circulation of the ideas goes on in man, calls the attention of his fellow-man to the ideas he is enjoying, so that his participation in such enjoyment. This is an indication from which each person can himself work out the other details as occasion demands. Further details are given in Appendix IV.

A World of Four Dimensions.—"*And I saw a new heaven and a new earth: . . . the holy city, new Jerusalem, . . . Having the glory of God: . . . and the city lieth foursquare. . . . And there shall be no more curse: But the throne of God and of the Lamb shall be in it.*" (Rev. 21, ver. 1, 2, 11, 10; and 22, ver. 3.)

Sec. I.

For some years, reasoning from the analogy of an imaginary two-dimensional being, conscious only of length and breadth, and unable to recognise height or depth, or anything above or below him, and therefore unconscious of the appearance of this three-dimensional world, various thinkers have suggested that there might be a world of four dimensions, of which the seeming three-dimensional man was equally unconscious.* It has been suggested by Mr. Wells that this fourth dimension is "Time." It may be more accurately expressed as spiritual infinity. Now heaven may be described mathematically as a world of four dimensions, wholly spiritual.† Everything that we see now as three-dimensional is only ethereal, namely, the real four-dimensional world seen wrongly from a false material standpoint, since the material man is only conscious of three dimensions of it, and that consciousness itself is false and absolutely misleading.‡

"If, therefore, we find the subject becomes more thinkable by assuming, say, a fourth-dimensional being than by following the ramifications of 'matter and force' into infinite space and time, we are quite justified in adopting the former method" § (E. Carpenter). Though doubtful assumption is better than nothing, definite knowledge is an absolute necessity for true progress.

In the same way that an imaginary two-dimensional being, appearing like a small, flat object, and only seeing the soles of your boots on the floor, would describe you as a straight line, say, 11 inches long, 3 inches wide, black, sometimes muddy, going about with a twin-brother—the fellow one—and constantly appearing and disappearing; so does the three-dimensional man describe his neighbour quite wrongly until he knows the truth. Should the two-dimensional being describe "the soles of the boots" as having no intelligence, no feeling, and being of little use, he would make the same mistake that we do if, talking of our fellow-man, we
273 8 describe him as an ignorant fool, or otherwise, as it is called, malpractise, that is, "think" in a derogatory way of him.

If the sharpened point of a pencil, held vertically, point upward, were placed by the side of this two-dimensional being, he would see it as a very short line. As the pencil was raised he would see this line increasing in length, and might speak of it as "growing." When the pencil had been sufficiently raised, he would see nothing,
279 44 and might speak of it as dead. So in this three-dimensional world

*See "Flat Land," by Dr. Abbott; "Another World," by A. T. Schofield, M.D.; "Scientific Romances," by C. H. Hinton; "Nature," May 1st, 1873, by G. F. Rodwell; "Messenger of Mathematics," 1891, Vol. XXI., p. 36, by W. W. Rouse Ball; "American Journal of Mathematics," 1880, Vol. III., p. 1, by Stringham. See also article in the "Wintonian," February, 1910, by R. A. T.; "The Art of Creation," by E. Carpenter; "A New Era of Thought," by C. H. Hinton; Professor Caley's Presidential Address to the British Association; Cajori's "History of Mathematics"; "Mathematical Recreations and Essays," by W. W. Rouse Ball; "Modern Views of Matter," by Sir William Crookes.

†"Christian Science translates Mind, God, to mortals. It is the Infinite Calculus defining the line, plane, space, and fourth dimension of Spirit" ("One Cause and Effect," "Misc. Writ.," p. 22. Mary Baker Eddy). See also "Science and Health," p. 575, line 21, by Mary Baker Eddy.

‡ § For notes, see next page.

Sec. I.

do we get a false sense of birth, growth, and death. Every tree, 274 40
for instance, as it apparently grows, is merely an exhibition of 281 31
certain phenomena, preconceived as material so-called facts, and
self-raised by the universal thought on the subject of vegetable 278 4
growth.

In a presidential address to the British Association, Professor Caley, the famous mathematician, declared his belief that every mathematical truth has an objective correlative in the world, that is, may actually describe a state of equilibrium. Taking, for instance, a suspension bridge, you can mathematically set out the tension of a wire, the pressure of the wind, the elasticity of the metal, etc. The truth at the back of Professor Caley's statement is one of the proofs that the fourth dimension exists, for this mathematical theory has been developed to a very considerable degree.

In the "Wintonian," of February, 1910, is an article on the Fourth Dimension, by R. A. T. He states: "To put it very briefly, the knowledge is a real and working knowledge, and the fourth dimension would enable us to move in defiance of the present known
limitations of space." So-called occult results are not, however, due 258 22
to action in four-dimensional space, as they merely exhibit the 261 43
phenomena of a three-dimensional world that are not generally cognised by the limited physical senses. Such results are solely concerned with matter in its finest, ethereal form, invisible under normal human conditions, and have nothing to do with the real world, heaven.

It is significant that C. H. Hinton, in his recent book, "A New Era of Thought," suggests that the birth, growth, life, and death
of animals are explainable by suggesting that an animal's life is 463 27
simply the phenomenon of a four-dimensional being passing through a three-dimensional world. This is interesting, because there is nothing to show that an animal may not be a limited sense of a real, spiritual being.

He also says: "After many years of work, during which the conception of four-dimensional bodies lay absolutely dark, at length, by a certain change of plan, the whole subject of four-dimensional existence became perfectly clear and easy to impart."*

The writer of the article in the "Wintonian" says: "I may say that I devoted no little time some years ago to an effort to comprehend the fourth dimension, according to Hinton's directions, but it was a failure."

All such efforts must prove failures whilst there is any confusion, 82 26
as in the case of Hinton, between— 262 6
(1.) The human, material, three-dimensional thought-forms that 18 19
Hinton recognised were all around us, although unseen by those who 300 32
are not psychic, that is, whose sight is not sufficiently developed, and,

(2.) The spiritual reality, of which these and all other material "thoughts" are but counterfeits.

‡ "The eye is not made to see everything. It picks out of the ocean of forms that which is accessible to it and believes this artificial limit to be the real limit. What we know of a living being is only a part of its real form. . . . Could our eyes see everything, a living being would appear to us as a cloud with changing contours" ("Evolution of Matter," p. 269. Dr. Le Bon).

§ "The Art of Creation," p. 8. ** "A New Era of Thought," p. 6.

The following short quotation from Cajori's "History of Mathematics" will express briefly some results of the fourth dimension, showing that the fourth-dimensional world cannot possibly be subject to material limitations. "Newcomb, the American astronomer, showed the possibility of turning a closed material shell inside out by simple flexure, without either stretching or tearing; Klein pointed out that in the fourth dimension knots could not be tied; Veronese showed that a body could be removed from a closed room without breaking the walls; C. S. Peirce proved that a body in four-dimensional space either rotates about two axes at once, or moves twists without losing one of its dimensions."

Mr. W. W. Rouse Ball, Fellow and Tutor of Trinity College, Cambridge, puts forward some interesting views with regard to a four-dimensional world, which he says "affords an explanation of some difficulties in our physical sciences."

At the end of last year, William Sidis, a boy aged 10, who appears to be a mathematical prodigy, delivered a lecture before the Harvard Mathematical Club, in which he put forward some new theories regarding the fourth dimension.

Sir William Crookes, F.R.S., writes: "To show how far we have been propelled on the strange new road, how dazzling are the wonders that display the researches, we have but to recall—Matter in a fourth state. ..."

These references will show how mathematicians are endeavouring to gain a knowledge of a fourth-dimensional world.

Counterfeits and Symbols.—"*The invisible things of him (God) from the creation of the world are clearly seen, being understood by the things that are made, even his eternal power and Godhead*" (Rom. ver. 20).

"*For Christ is not entered into the holy places made with hands, which are the figures of the true; but into heaven itself*" (Heb. 9, v. 24).

Man is spiritual and four-dimensional. The apparent material man is not real, but is purely illusionary. "The ideal, after all, is truer than the real, for the ideal is the eternal element in perishable things; it is their type, their sum, their raison d'être" (Amiel). "And things are not what they seem" (Longfellow). "Matter, motion, and force, are not the reality, but the symbols of reality" (Herbert Spencer).

A material world of three dimensions only is visible to the material senses; consequently everything about you is simply something connected with your spiritual self seen falsely, seen

---

materially, a counterfeit of the spiritual reality." "There is a natural body, and there is a spiritual body. ... The first man is of the earth, earthy; the second man is the Lord from heaven" (I. Cor. 15, ver. 44, 47). "We have a building of God, an house not made with hands, eternal in the heavens" (II. Cor. 5, ver. 1).

Charles Kingsley said: "The belief is coming every day stronger with me that all symmetrical objects are types of some spiritual truth or existence. Everything seems to be full of God's refrain, if we could but see it. Oh! to see, if but for a moment, the whole in harmony of the great system; to hear once the music that the whole ... makes as it performs His bidding."

Plato, in the "Phaedrus" says: "The higher qualities which are precious in souls ... are seen through a glass dimly; and they are few who, going to the images, behold in them the realities, and they only with difficulty."

Professor Drummond said: "Nature ... is a working model of the spiritual. It is a very poor counterfeit model."

"The world constructed with the impressions of our senses is a summary translation, and necessarily a far from faithful one of the real world which we know not"? (Dr. G. Le Bon).

All must gain the knowledge of the real man, of our real selves. "So in man's self arise august anticipations, symbols, types, of a dim splendour, ever on before" (R. Browning). The Revelator, seeing in advance what is about to happen, writes: "The kingdoms of this world are become the kingdoms of our Lord" (Rev. 11, ver. 15).

"Upon the heights we see that every act and every thought are infallibly bound up with something great and immortal" (Maeterlinck).

"For anything that may be proved to the contrary, there may be a real something which is the cause of all our impressions; that something, though not likenesses, are symbols of that something; and that the part of that something, which we call the nervous system, is an apparatus for supplying us with a sort of algebra of ... fact, based on those symbols" (Professor Huxley).

The something that Huxley so indubitably searched after has ... been proved to be God, the Principle of all good, the great I AM, Mind, Spirit, Soul, Life, Truth, and Love, all substance, intelligence, and the only cause.

Swedenborg spoke of correspondences, but confined himself within a false belief in spirit appearances, as is clear from his writings that he thought the spiritual world was visible around us under certain material conditions. He had not learned that the things seen by him, which he thought were spiritual, were merely materialised thoughts" in their more ethereal and less tangible ...

"Every creation or idea of Spirit has its counterfeit in some material-...

Sec. I.

NATURAL LAWS MERELY MEMORIA TECHNICA.

THE ADVANCEMENT OF HUMAN KNOWLEDGE.

CPSIA information can be obtained
at www.ICGtesting.com
Printed in the USA
LVHW081920261121
704539LV00014B/1426

9 781015 336476